I0429360

Nobel Quotes

Inspiring and Perplexing Quotes of Nobel Prize Winners

Table of Contents

Physiology or Medicine Nobel Laureates   77

Chemistry Nobel Laureates   91

Physics Nobel Laureates   109

Legal

I, the collector of these quotes, am not affiliated with the Nobel Prize, the Nobel Foundation or any Nobel Laureates.

Disclaimer: To the best of my knowledge, all quotations included here fall under the fair use or public domain guidelines of copyright law in the United States. If you believe that any quotation violates a copyright you hold or represent, I will immediately remove it from new copies of the book upon notification pending good-faith resolution of any dispute.

Copyright of non public domain quotes belongs to their respective authors and translators. All other work copyright is upheld.

© 2012-11-23, György Chityil, Budapest, Hungary

Special Thanks to the Nobel Foundation

I would like to express my gratitude for the Nobel Foundation for granting me permission to write this book. I quote from Nobel Laureate speeches extensively, and also use photos of Nobel Laureates from http://nobelprize.org.

Individuals Appearing on the Cover, and Photo Sources

From left to right

1. Row
   1. "Gabriel García Márquez - Biography". Nobelprize.org. 1 Nov 2012
      http://www.nobelprize.org/nobel_prizes/literature/laureates/1982/marquez.html
   2. "Dorothy Crowfoot Hodgkin - Biography". Nobelprize.org. 1 Nov 2012
      http://www.nobelprize.org/nobel_prizes/chemistry/laureates/1964/hodgkin.html
   3. "Kofi Annan - Biography". Nobelprize.org. 1 Nov 2012
      http://www.nobelprize.org/nobel_prizes/peace/laureates/2001/annan.html
   4. "Liu Xiaobo - Biographical". Nobelprize.org. 1 Nov 2012
      http://www.nobelprize.org/nobel_prizes/peace/laureates/2010/xiaobo.html
   5. "Willy Brandt - Curriculum Vitae". Nobelprize.org. 1 Nov 2012
      http://www.nobelprize.org/nobel_prizes/peace/laureates/1971/brandt.html
2. Row
   1. "Barack H. Obama - Biographical". Nobelprize.org. 30 Oct 2012
      http://www.nobelprize.org/nobel_prizes/peace/laureates/2009/obama.html
      Photo: Pete Souza, Obama-Biden Transition Project, licensed by Attribution Share Alike 3.0
   2. "Mother Teresa - Biography". Nobelprize.org. 30 Oct 2012
      http://www.nobelprize.org/nobel_prizes/peace/laureates/1979/teresa.html
   3. "Albert Einstein - Biography". Nobelprize.org. 30 Oct 2012
      http://www.nobelprize.org/nobel_prizes/physics/laureates/1921/einstein.html
   4. "Wangari Maathai - Biography". Nobelprize.org. 1 Nov 2012
      http://www.nobelprize.org/nobel_prizes/peace/laureates/2004/maathai.html
   5. "Pablo Neruda - Biography". Nobelprize.org. 1 Nov 2012
      http://www.nobelprize.org/nobel_prizes/literature/laureates/1971/neruda.html
3. Row
   1. "Albert Camus - Biography". Nobelprize.org. 1 Nov 2012
      http://www.nobelprize.org/nobel_prizes/literature/laureates/1957/camus.html
   2. "Alva Myrdal - Biography". Nobelprize.org. 1 Nov 2012
      http://www.nobelprize.org/nobel_prizes/peace/laureates/1982/myrdal.html
   3. "William Butler Yeats - Biography". Nobelprize.org. 1 Nov 2012
      http://www.nobelprize.org/nobel_prizes/literature/laureates/1923/yeats.html
   4. "Pearl Buck - Biography". Nobelprize.org. 1 Nov 2012
      http://www.nobelprize.org/nobel_prizes/literature/laureates/1938/buck.html
   5. "André Gide - Biography". Nobelprize.org. 1 Nov 2012
      http://www.nobelprize.org/nobel_prizes/literature/laureates/1947/gide.html
4. Row
   1. "Samuel Beckett - Curriculum Vitae". Nobelprize.org. 1 Nov 2012
      http://www.nobelprize.org/nobel_prizes/literature/laureates/1969/beckett.html
   2. "Rita Levi-Montalcini - Autobiography". Nobelprize.org. 1 Nov 2012
      http://www.nobelprize.org/nobel_prizes/medicine/laureates/1986/levi-montalcini.html

3. "Henri Becquerel - Biography". Nobelprize.org. 1 Nov 2012
   http://www.nobelprize.org/nobel_prizes/physics/laureates/1903/becquerel.html
4. "Mairead Corrigan - Curriculum Vitae". Nobelprize.org. 1 Nov 2012
   http://www.nobelprize.org/nobel_prizes/peace/laureates/1976/corrigan.html
5. "Alexandr Solzhenitsyn - Autobiography". Nobelprize.org. 1 Nov 2012
   http://www.nobelprize.org/nobel_prizes/literature/laureates/1970/solzhenitsyn.html

Introduction

Since 1901, hundreds of outstanding individuals, such as Albert Einstein, Mother Theresa, and Barack Obama received the Nobel Prize for advancing the experience of our existence in five different categories: peace, literature, physics, chemistry, physiology or medicine and economics. This book collects their wondrous thoughts and sayings, so you may glance into some of the greatest minds who will not just inspire, but uplift, entertain, or even perplex you. You can draw inspiration from their unfazed attitudes, heighten your thoughts with their extraordinary understanding, and laugh with their sharp wit. I sifted through thousands of words in order to bring you the most enjoyable thoughts common to humanity, and my limiting the selection to Nobel winners ensures you read the best quotes.

Enjoy the reading!

Literature Nobel Laureates

Rudyard Kipling

Prize Motivation: "*in consideration of the power of observation, originality of imagination, virility of ideas and remarkable talent for narration which characterize the creations of this world-famous author*"
Prize Year: *1907*
Prize Category: *Literature*
Source: nobelprize.org

Words are, of course, the most powerful drug used by mankind.
Rudyard Kipling Speech, quoted in The Times (February 15, 1923).

Originally the cliffs and their approaches must have been pretty, but they have been so carefully defiled with advertisements that they are now one big blistered abomination.
American Notes by Rudyard Kipling

Men can 'most always tell when a man has handled things for himself, and then they treat him as one of themselves.
Captains Courageous by Rudyard Kipling

...after you've made a mistake—ye don't make fewer'n a hundred a day—the next best thing's to own up to it like men.
Captains Courageous by Rudyard Kipling

I am afraid to be kicked, but I am not afraid to die, because I know what I know. You are not afraid to be kicked, but you are afraid to die.
Indian Tales by Rudyard Kipling

...the western world which clings to the dread of death more closely than the hope of life...
Indian Tales by Rudyard Kipling

There are few things sweeter in this world than the guileless, hot-headed, intemperate, open admiration of a junior. Even a woman in her blindest devotion does not fall into the gait of the man she adores, tilt her bonnet to the angle at which he wears his hat, or interlard her speech with his pet oaths.
Indian Tales by Rudyard Kipling

Terrible women would invent unclean variants of the men's belief for the elevation of their sisters.
Indian Tales by Rudyard Kipling

If men had not this delusion as to the ultra-importance of their own particular employments, I suppose that they would sit down and kill themselves.
Indian Tales by Rudyard Kipling

All India is full of holy men stammering gospels in strange tongues; shaken and consumed in the fires of their own zeal; dreamers, babblers, and visionaries: as it has been from the beginning and will continue to the end.
Kim by Rudyard Kipling

There are many lies in the world, and not a few liars, but there are no liars like our bodies, except it be the sensations of our bodies.
Kim by Rudyard Kipling

Take my word for it, the silliest woman can manage a clever man; but it needs a very clever woman to manage a fool.
Plain Tales from the Hills by Rudyard Kipling

Too much work and too much energy kill a man just as effectively as too much assorted vice or too much drink.
Plain Tales from the Hills by Rudyard Kipling

Never praise a sister to a sister, in the hope of your compliments reaching the proper ears, and so preparing the way for you later on. Sisters are women first, and sisters afterwards; and you will find that you do yourself harm.
Plain Tales from the Hills (1888) - False Dawn Rudyard Kipling

Yet all my wanderings had shown me one sure thing, which is, that a King without money is like a spear without a head. He cannot do much harm.
Puck of Pook's Hill by Rudyard Kipling

The curses of a fool and the dust of a journey are two things no wise man can escape.
Puck of Pook's Hill by Rudyard Kipling

It is the hardest thing in the world to frighten a mongoose, because he is eaten up from nose to tail with curiosity.
Rikki-Tikki-Tavi by Rudyard Kipling

The Law of the Jungle, which never orders anything without a reason, forbids every beast to eat Man except when he is killing to show his children how to kill, and then he must hunt outside the hunting grounds of his pack or tribe.
The Jungle Book by Rudyard Kipling

'Better he should be bruised from head to foot by me who love him than that he should come to harm through ignorance,' Baloo answered very earnestly.
The Jungle Book by Rudyard Kipling

Where he had looked for love, she gave him first aversion and then hate.
The Light That Failed by Rudyard Kipling

When little boys have learned a new bad word they are never happy till they have chalked it up on a door. And this also is Literature.
The Phantom Rickshaw and Other Ghost Stories by Rudyard Kipling

Do you know what fear is? Not ordinary fear of insult, injury or death, but abject, quivering dread of something that you cannot see—fear that dries the inside of the mouth and half of the throat—fear that makes you sweat on the palms of the hands, and gulp in order to keep the uvula at work? This is a fine Fear—a great cowardice, and must be felt to be appreciated.
The Phantom Rickshaw and Other Ghost Stories by Rudyard Kipling

Hathi never does anything till the time comes, and that is one of the reasons why he lives so long.
The Second Jungle Book by Rudyard Kipling

Rabindranath Tagore

Prize Motivation: "*because of his profoundly sensitive, fresh and beautiful verse, by which, with consummate skill, he has made his poetic thought, expressed in his own English words, a part of the literature of the West*"
Prize Year: *1913*
Prize Category: *Literature*
Source: nobelprize.org

Where the mind is without fear and the head is held high; Where knowledge is free; Where the world has not been broken up into fragments by narrow domestic walls; Where words come out from the depth of truth; Where tireless striving stretches its arms towards perfection; Where the clear stream of reason has not lost its way into the dreary desert sand of dead habit; Where the mind is led forward by thee into ever-widening thought and action-- Into that heaven of freedom, my Father, let my country awake.
Gitanjali by Rabindranath Tagore

The traveller has to knock at every alien door to come to his own, and one has to wander through all the outer worlds to reach the innermost shrine at the end. My eyes strayed far and wide before I shut them and said 'Here art thou!'
Gitanjali by Rabindranath Tagore

The real truth is that science is not man's nature, it is mere knowledge and training. By knowing the laws of the material universe you do not change your deeper humanity. You can borrow knowledge from others, but you cannot borrow temperament.
Nationalism by Rabindranath Tagore

When a man does not realise his kinship with the world, he lives in a prison-house whose walls are alien to him.
Sadhana : the realisation of life by Rabindranath Tagore

To understand anything is to find in it something which is our own, and it is the discovery of ourselves outside us which makes us glad. This relation of understanding is partial, but the relation of love is complete. In love the sense of difference is obliterated and the human soul fulfils its purpose in perfection, transcending the limits of itself and reaching across the threshold of the infinite. Therefore love is the highest bliss that man can attain to, for through it alone he truly knows that he is more than himself, and that he is at one with the All.
Sadhana : The Realisation of Life by Rabindranath Tagore

To understand anything is to find in it something which is our own, and it is the discovery of ourselves outside us which makes us glad.
Sadhana-The Realization of Life by Rabindranath Tagore

We never cared for such useless things as knowledge. We only cared for truth.
Stories from Tagore by Rabindranath Tagore

The thing that made a seven-year-old boy's heart go thump, thump with delight was this one sovereign truth, this reality of all realities: "Once there was a king."
Stories from Tagore by Rabindranath Tagore

If you shed tears when you miss the sun, you also miss the stars.
Stray Birds by Rabindranath Tagore

Every child comes with the message that God is not yet discouraged of man.
Stray Birds by Rabindranath Tagore

A mind all logic is like a knife all blade. It makes the hand bleed that uses it.
Stray Birds by Rabindranath Tagore

To be outspoken is easy when you do not wait to speak the complete truth.
Stray Birds by Rabindranath Tagore

God may grant us gifts, but the merit of being able to take and hold them must be our own. Alas for the boons that slip through unworthy hands!
The Home and the World by Rabindranath Tagore

Purity, they imagined, was only becoming in those on whom fortune had not smiled. It is the moon which has room for stains, not the stars.
The Home and the World by Rabindranath Tagore

Perfect gain is the best of all; but if that is impossible, then the next best gain is perfect losing.
The Home and the World by Rabindranath Tagore

Woman knows man well enough where he is weak, but she is quite unable to fathom him where he is strong. The fact is that man is as much a mystery to woman as woman is to man. If that were not so, the separation of the sexes would only have been a waste of Nature's energy.
The Home and the World by Rabindranath Tagore

'Neither am I divine: I am human. And therefore I dare not permit the evil which is in me to be exaggerated into an image of my country – never, never!'
The Home and the World by Rabindranath Tagore

Can there be any real happiness for a woman in merely feeling that she has power over a man?

The Home and the World by Rabindranath Tagore

The Geography of a country is not the whole truth. No one can give up his life for a map!

The Home and the World by Rabindranath Tagore

William Butler Yeats

Prize Motivation: "*for his always inspired poetry, which in a highly artistic form gives expression to the spirit of a whole nation*"
Prize Year: *1923*
Prize Category: *Literature*
Source: nobelprize.org

I would spread the cloths under your feet:
But I, being poor, have only my dreams;
I have spread my dreams under your feet;
Tread softly because you tread on my dreams.

Aedh Wishes for the Cloths of Heaven by W. B. (William Butler) Yeats

I learned from the people themselves, before I learned it from any book, that they cannot separate the idea of an art or a craft from the idea of a cult with ancient technicalities and mysteries. They can hardly separate mere learning from witchcraft, and are fond of words and verses that keep half their secret to themselves.
Ideas of Good and Evil by W. B. (William Butler) Yeats

I think that all noble things are the result of warfare; great nations and classes, of warfare in the visible world, great poetry and philosophy, of invisible warfare, the division of a mind within itself, a victory, the sacrifice of a man to himself.
Synge and the Ireland of His Time by W. B. (William Butler) Yeats

Let us go forth, the tellers of tales, and seize whatever prey the heart long for, and have no fear. Everything exists, everything is true, and the earth is only a little dust under our feet.
The Celtic Twilight by W. B. (William Butler) Yeats

What is literature but the expression of moods by the vehicle of symbol and incident?
The Celtic Twilight by W. B. (William Butler) Yeats

No human soul is like any other human soul, and therefore the love of God for any human soul is infinite, for no other soul can satisfy the same need in God.
The Celtic Twilight by W. B. (William Butler) Yeats

...there are three things that are the gift of the Almighty--poetry and dancing and principles.
The Celtic Twilight by W. B. (William Butler) Yeats

Hope and Memory have one daughter and her name is Art, and she has built her dwelling far from the desperate field where men hang out their garments upon forked boughs to be banners of battle. O beloved daughter of Hope and Memory, be with me for a little.
The Celtic Twilight by W. B. (William Butler) Yeats

Everything exists, everything is true, and the earth is only a little dust under our feet.
The Celtic Twilight by W. B. (William Butler) Yeats

And yet the beauties that I loved
Are in my memory;
I spit into the face of Time
That has transfigured me.
The Lamentation Of The Old Pensioner by W. B. (William Butler) Yeats

I on the other hand believe that poetry and romance cannot be made by the most conscientious study of famous moments and of the thoughts and feelings of others, but only by looking into that little, infinite, faltering, eternal flame that we call ourselves.
The Secret Rose by W. B. (William Butler) Yeats

...no shining candelabra have prevented us from looking into the darkness, and when one looks into the darkness there is always something there.
The Secret Rose by W. B. (William Butler) Yeats

George Bernard Shaw

Prize Motivation: "*for his work which is marked by both idealism and humanity, its stimulating satire often being infused with a singular poetic beauty*"
Prize Year: *1925*
Prize Category: *Literature*
Source: nobelprize.org

People always grow tired of one another. I grow tired of myself whenever I am left alone for ten minutes, and I am certain that I am fonder of myself than anyone can be of another person.
An Unsocial Socialist by George Bernard Shaw

Beer is the chloroform that enables the laborer to endure the severe operation of living; that is why we can always assure one another over our wine that the rascal's misery is due to his habit of drinking.
An Unsocial Socialist by George Bernard Shaw

Below them are two notable drawbacks of civilization: a palace, and soldiers.
Caesar and Cleopatra by George Bernard Shaw

There is no more dangerous mistake than the mistake of supposing that we cannot have too much of a good thing.
Getting Married by George Bernard Shaw

The respectable men all regarded the marriage ceremony as a rite which absolved them from the laws of health and temperance; inaugurated a life-long honeymoon; and placed their pleasures on exactly the same footing as their prayers.
Getting Married by George Bernard Shaw

When your heart is broken, your boats are burned: nothing matters any more. It is the end of happiness and the beginning of peace.
Heartbreak House by George Bernard Shaw

Old-fashioned people think you can have a soul without money. They think the less money you have, the more soul you have. Young people nowadays know better. A soul is a very expensive thing to keep: much more so than a motor car.
Heartbreak House by George Bernard Shaw

It's prudent to gain the whole world and lose your own soul. But don't forget that your soul sticks to you if you stick to it; but the world has a way of slipping through your fingers.
Heartbreak House by George Bernard Shaw

The only man who behaved sensibly was my tailor: he took my measure anew every time he saw me, whilst all the rest went on with their old measurements and expected them to fit me.
Man and Superman by George Bernard Shaw

The true artist will let his wife starve, his children go barefoot, his mother drudge for his living at seventy, sooner than work at anything but his art.
Man and Superman by George Bernard Shaw

Beware of the pursuit of the Superhuman: it leads to an indiscriminate contempt for the Human.
Man and Superman by George Bernard Shaw

I tell you, the first duty of manhood and womanhood is a Declaration of Independence: the man who pleads his father's authority is no man: the woman who pleads her mother's authority is unfit to bear citizens to a free people.
Man and Superman by George Bernard Shaw

People are always blaming circumstances for what they are. I don't believe in circumstances. The people who get on in this world are the people who get up and look for the circumstances they want, and, if they can't find them, make them.
Mrs. Warren's Profession by George Bernard Shaw

Well, of course, dearie, it's only good manners to be ashamed of it: it's expected from a woman. Women have to pretend to feel a great deal that they don't feel.
Mrs. Warren's Profession by George Bernard Shaw

All censorships exist to prevent anyone from challenging current conceptions and existing institutions. All progress is initiated by challenging current concepts, and executed by supplanting existing institutions. Consequently the first condition of progress is the removal of censorships. There is the whole case against censorships in a nutshell.
Mrs. Warren's Profession by George Bernard Shaw

But I can't stand saying one thing when everyone knows I mean another. Whats the use in such hypocrisy? If people arrange the world that way for women, theres no good pretending it's arranged the other way.
Mrs. Warren's Profession by George Bernard Shaw

Remember that you are a human being with a soul and the divine gift of articulate speech: that your native language is the language of Shakespear and Milton and The Bible; and don't sit there crooning like a bilious pigeon.
Pygmalion by George Bernard Shaw

If you can't appreciate what you've got, you'd better get what you can appreciate.
Pygmalion by George Bernard Shaw

A little learning is a dangerous thing; Drink deep; or taste not the Pierian spring.
The Doctor's Dilemma by George Bernard Shaw

The secret of being miserable is to have leisure to bother about whether you are happy or not. The cure for it is occupation, because occupation means pre-occupation; and the pre-occupied person is neither happy nor unhappy, but simply alive and active, which is pleasanter than any happiness until you are tired of it.
Treatise on Parents and Children by George Bernard Shaw

Thomas Mann

Prize Motivation: "*principally for his great novel, Buddenbrooks, which has won steadily increased recognition as one of the classic works of contemporary literature*"
Prize Year: *1929*
Prize Category: *Literature*
Source: *nobelprize.org*

We are not born, my dear daughter, to pursue our own small personal happiness, for we are not separate, independent, self-subsisting individuals, but links in a chain; and it is inconceivable that we would be what we are without those who have preceded us and shown us the path that they themselves have scrupulously trod,
Buddenbrooks: The Decline of a Family by Thomas Mann

Because man loves and honors man as long as he is not able to judge him, and desire is a product of lacking knowledge.
Death in Venice by Thomas Mann

The happiness of writers is the thought that can be entirely emotion and the emotion that can be entirely thought.
Death in Venice by Thomas Mann

Almost every artistic individual has a luxurious and treacherous propensity to recognize beauty-creating inequity and to render homage to aristocratic entitlement.
Death in Venice by Thomas Mann

For a man loves and respects his fellow man only insofar as he is unable to assess him, and longing is a product of insufficient knowledge.
Death in Venice by Thomas Mann

To repose in perfection is the desire of all those who strive for excellence, and is not nothingness a form of perfection?
Death in Venice by Thomas Mann

Solitude begets originality, bold and disconcerting beauty, poetry. But solitude can also beget perversity, disparity, the absurd and the forbidden.
Death in Venice by Thomas Mann

For a major product of the intellect to make an immediate broad and deep impact it must rest upon a secret affinity, indeed, a congruence between the personal destiny of its author and the collective destiny of his generation.
Death in Venice by Thomas Mann

Thought that can merge wholly into feeling, feeling that can merge wholly into thought—these are the artist's highest joy.

Death in Venice and Seven Other Stories by Thomas Mann

Passion is like crime: it does not thrive on the established order and the common round; it welcomes every blow dealt the bourgeois structure, every weakening of the social fabric, because therein it feels a sure hope of its own advantage.

Death in Venice and Seven Other Stories by Thomas Mann

What is freedom? Only the neutral is free. The characteristic is never free, it is stamped, determined, bound.

Doctor Faustus. The Life of the German composer Adrian Leverkühn, told by a friend by Thomas Mann

Music was actually the most intellectual of all the arts, as was evident from the fact that in it, as in no other, form and content are interwoven and absolutely one and the same.

Doctor Faustus. The Life of the German composer Adrian Leverkühn, told by a friend by Thomas Mann

Sinclair Lewis

Prize Motivation: "*for his vigorous and graphic art of description and his ability to create, with wit and humour, new types of characters*"
Prize Year: *1930*
Prize Category: *Literature*
Source: nobelprize.org

God give me unclouded eyes and freedom from haste. God give me a quiet and relentless anger against all pretense and all pretentious work and all work left slack and unfinished. God give me a restlessness whereby I may neither sleep nor accept praise till my observed results equal my calculated results or in pious glee I discover and assault my error. God give me strength not to trust to God!
Arrowsmith by Sinclair Lewis

He is the only real revolutionary, the authentic scientist, because he alone knows how liddle he knows.
Arrowsmith by Sinclair Lewis

In the study of the profession to which he had looked forward all his life he found irritation and vacuity as well as serene wisdom; he saw no one clear path to Truth but a thousand paths to a thousand truths far-off and doubtful.
Arrowsmith by Sinclair Lewis

It is one of the major tragedies that nothing is more discomforting than the hearty affection of the Old Friends who never were friends.
Arrowsmith by Sinclair Lewis

He insisted that there is no Truth but only many truths; that Truth is not a colored bird to be chased among the rocks and captured by its tail, but a skeptical attitude toward life.
Arrowsmith by Sinclair Lewis

You know it's almost impossible to get people to read the Bible honestly. They've been so brought up to take the church interpretation of every word that they read into it whatever they've been taught to find there.
Elmer Gantry by Sinclair Lewis

Why is that it's only in religion that the things you got to believe are agin all experience?
Elmer Gantry by Sinclair Lewis

Which is worse, not to tip when a tip has been expected; or to tip, when the tip is an insult?
Free Air by Sinclair Lewis

"But I want to do something with life." "What's better than making a comfy home and bringing up some cute kids and knowing nice homey people?" It was the immemorial male reply to the restless woman.
Main Street by Sinclair Lewis

Such a society functions admirably in the large production of cheap automobiles, dollar watches, and safety razors. But it is not satisfied until the entire world also admits that the end and joyous purpose of living is to ride in flivvers, to make advertising-pictures of dollar watches, and in the twilight to sit talking not of love and courage but of the convenience of safety razors.
Main Street by Sinclair Lewis

A girl on a hilltop; credulous, plastic, young; drinking the air as she longed to drink life. The eternal aching comedy of expectant youth.
Main Street by Sinclair Lewis

Luigi Pirandello

Prize Motivation: "*for his bold and ingenious revival of dramatic and scenic art*"
Prize Year: *1934*
Prize Category: *Literature*
Source: nobelprize.org

Anyone can be heroic from time to time, but a gentleman is something which you have to be all the time. Which isn't easy.
The Pleasure of Honesty by Luigi Pirandello, trans. William Murray

What's the cause of our ills and sadness? Democracy, my dear sir, democracy! Government by the majority! When power is in the hands of one man, he knows that it's his job to satisfy many; but when many govern they all think of satisfying themselves. And what do we get? Tyranny, my dear sir, in its most stupid form: tyranny masked as liberty!
Il fu Mattia Pascal (Mondadori) by Pirandello Luigi

For man never reasons so much and becomes so introspective as when he suffers; since he is anxious to get at the cause of his sufferings, to learn who has produced them, and whether it is just or unjust that he should have to bear them. On the other hand, when he is happy, he takes his happiness as it comes and doesn't analyze it, just as if happiness were his right.
Six Characters in Search of an Author by Luigi Pirandello, trans. Edward Storer

Oh sir, you know well that life is full of infinite absurdities, which, strangely enough, do not even need to appear plausible, since they are true.
Six Characters in Search of an Author by Luigi Pirandello, trans. Edward Storer

A character, sir, may always ask a man who he is. Because a character has really a life of his own, marked with his especial characteristics; for which reason he is always "somebody." But a man -- I'm not speaking of you now -- may very well be "nobody."
Six Characters in Search of an Author by Luigi Pirandello, trans. Edward Storer

But a fact is like a sack which won't stand up when it is empty. In order that it may stand up, one has to put into it the reason and sentiment which have caused it to exist.
Six Characters in Search of an Author by Luigi Pirandello, trans. Edward Storer

Illusions of reality represented in this fatuous comedy of life that never ends, nor can ever end! Because if tomorrow it were to end . . . then why, all would be finished.
Six Characters in Search of an Author by Luigi Pirandello, trans. Edward Storer

But don't you see that the whole trouble lies here. In words, words. Each one of us has within him a whole world of things, each man of us his own special world. And how can we ever come to an understanding if I put in the words I utter the sense and value of things as I see them; while you who listen to me must inevitably translate them according to the conception of things each one of you has within himself. We think we understand each other, but we never really do.
Six Characters in Search of an Author by Luigi Pirandello

When faith is lacking, it becomes impossible to create certain states of happiness, for we lack the necessary humility.
Six Characters in Search of an Author by Luigi Pirandello

And this was a real crime, sir; because he who has had the luck to be born a character can laugh even at death. He cannot die. The man, the writer, the instrument of the creation will die, but his creation does not die. And to live for ever, it does not need to have extraordinary gifts or to be able to work wonders.
Six Characters in Search of an Author by Luigi Pirandello

Hermann Hesse

Prize Motivation: "*for his inspired writings which, while growing in boldness and penetration, exemplify the classical humanitarian ideals and high qualities of style*"
Prize Year: *1946*
Prize Category: *Literature*
Source: nobelprize.org

If you hate a person, you hate something in him that is part of yourself. What isn't part of ourselves doesn't disturb us.
Demian: The Story of Emil Sinclair's Youth (1919), first published under the pseudonym "Emil Sinclair"

Only the ideas that we actually live are of any value
Demian: The Story of Emil Sinclair's Youth (1919), first published under the pseudonym "Emil Sinclair"

Passion is always a mystery and unaccountable, and unfortunately there is no doubt that life does not spare its purest children and often it is just the most deserving people who cannot help loving those that destroy them.
Gertrude (1910) As translated by Hilda Rosner

If what matters in a person's existence is to accept the inevitable consciously, to taste the good and bad to the full and to make for oneself a more individual, unaccidental and inward destiny alongside one's external fate, then my life has been neither empty nor worthless.
Gertrude (1910) As translated by Hilda Rosner

Oh, love isn't there to make us happy. I believe it exists to show us how much we can endure.
Peter Camenzind (1904)

When someone is searching," said Siddhartha, "then it might easily happen that the only thing his eyes still see is that what he searches for, that he is unable to find anything, to let anything enter his mind, because he always thinks of nothing but the object of his search, because he has a goal, because he is obsessed by the goal. Searching means: having a goal. But finding means: being free, being open, having no goal. You, oh venerable one, are perhaps indeed a searcher, because, striving for your goal, there are many things you don't see, which are directly in front of your eyes.
Siddhartha by Hermann Hesse

Most of all, he learned from it to listen, to pay close attention with a quiet heart, with a waiting, opened soul, without passion, without a wish, without judgement, without an opinion.
Siddhartha by Hermann Hesse

Writing is good, thinking is better. Being smart is good, being patient is better.
Siddhartha by Hermann Hesse

But I think it is only important to love the world, not to despise it, not for us to hate each other, but to be able to regard the world and ourselves and all beings with love, admiration and respect.
Siddhartha by Hermann Hesse

All birth means separation from the All, the confinement within limitation, the separation from God, the pangs of being born ever anew. The return into the All, the dissolution of painful individuation, the reunion with God means the expansion of the soul until it is able once more to embrace the All.
Steppenwolf by Hermann Hesse

Thomas Stearns Eliot

Prize Motivation: "*for his outstanding, pioneer contribution to present-day poetry*"
Prize Year: *1948*
Prize Category: *Literature*
Source: nobelprize.org

Only those who will risk going too far can possibly find out how far one can go.
Uknown

To do the useful thing, to say the courageous thing, to contemplate the beautiful thing: that is enough for one man's life.
The Use of Poetry and the Use of Criticism

In the work of every poet there will certainly be much that can only appeal to those who inhabit the same region, or speak the same language, as the poet. But nevertheless there is a meaning to the phrase «the poetry of Europe», and even to the word «poetry» the world over. I think that in poetry people of different countries and different languages - though it be apparently only through a small minority in any one country - acquire an understanding of each other which, however partial, is still essential.
"T.S. Eliot - Banquet Speech". Nobelprize.org. 15 Nov 2012

...while language constitutes a barrier, poetry itself gives us a reason for trying to overcome the barrier. To enjoy poetry belonging to another language, is to enjoy an understanding of the people to whom that language belongs, an understanding we can get in no other way.
"T.S. Eliot - Banquet Speech". Nobelprize.org. 15 Nov 2012

I believe that the choice before us is between the formation of a new Christian culture, and the acceptance of a pagan one.
Christianity And Culture by T. S. Eliot

Words are perhaps the hardest of all material of art: for they must be used to express both visual beauty and beauty of sound, as well as communicating a grammatical statement.
Ezra Pound: His Metric and Poetry by T. S. (Thomas Stearns) Eliot

The only kind of emotion worthy of a poet is the inspirational emotion which energises and strengthens, and which is very remote from the everyday emotion of sloppiness and sentiment....
Ezra Pound: His Metric and Poetry by T. S. (Thomas Stearns) Eliot

The only wisdom we can hope to acquire Is the wisdom of humility: humility is endless.
Four Quartets (Faber Poetry) by T.S. Eliot

Love is most nearly itself When here and now cease to matter.
Four Quartets (Faber Poetry) by T.S. Eliot

human kind Cannot bear very much reality. Time past and time future What might have been and what has been Point to one end, which is always present.
Four Quartets (Faber Poetry) by T.S. Eliot

I grow old . . . I grow old . . .
I shall wear the bottoms of my trousers rolled.
The Love Song of J. Alfred Prufrock by T. S. Eliot

Do I dare
Disturb the universe?
In a minute there is time
For decisions and revisions which a minute will reverse.
The Love Song of J. Alfred Prufrock by T. S. Eliot

I will show you something different from either
Your shadow at morning striding behind you
Or your shadow at evening rising to meet you;
I will show you fear in a handful of dust.
The Waste Land by T. S. Eliot

April is the cruellest month, breeding Lilacs out of the dead land, mixing Memory and desire, stirring Dull roots with spring rain.
The Waste Land by Thomas Stearns Eliot

William Faulkner

Prize Motivation: *"for his powerful and artistically unique contribution to the modern American novel"*
Prize Year: *1949*
Prize Category: *Literature*
Source: nobelprize.org

I believe that man will not merely endure: he will prevail. He is immortal, not because he alone among creatures has an inexhaustible voice, but because he has a soul, a spirit capable of compassion and sacrifice and endurance.
"William Faulkner - Banquet Speech". Nobelprize.org. 17 Nov 2012

... my work - a life's work in the agony and sweat of the human spirit, not for glory and least of all for profit, but to create out of the materials of the human spirit something which did not exist before.
"William Faulkner - Banquet Speech". Nobelprize.org. 17 Nov 2012

Or maybe women are even less complex than that and to them any wedding is better than no wedding and a big wedding with a villain preferable to a small one with a saint.
Absalom, Absalom! by William Faulkner

It takes two people to make you, and one people to die. That's how the world is going to end.
As I Lay Dying by William Faulkner

I can remember how when I was young I believed death to be a phenomenon of the body; now I know it to be merely a function of the mind—and that of the minds of the ones who suffer the bereavement. The nihilists say it is the end; the fundamentalists, the beginning; when in reality it is no more than a single tenant or family moving out of a tenement or a town.
As I Lay Dying by William Faulkner

I notice how it takes a lazy man, a man that hates moving, to get set on moving once he does get started off, the same as he was set on staying still, like it aint the moving he hates so much as the starting and the stopping.
As I Lay Dying by William Faulkner

Be scared. You cant help that. But dont be afraid. Aint nothing in the woods going to hurt you if you dont corner it or it dont smell that you are afraid. A bear or a deer has got to be scared of a coward the same as a brave man has got to be.
Go Down, Moses by William Faulkner

No wonder the ruined woods I used to know dont cry for retribution! The people who have destroyed it will accomplish its revenge.
Go Down, Moses by William Faulkner

Memory believes before knowing remembers. Believes longer than recollects, longer than knowing even wonders.
Light in August by William Faulkner

Surely, if there are two professions in which there should be no professional jealousy, they are prostitution and literature.
New Orleans Sketches by William Faulkner

There are things, circumstances, conditions in the world which should not be there but are, and you cant escape them and indeed, you would not escape them even if you had the choice, since they too are a part of Motion, of participating in life, being alive. But they should arrive with grace, decency. I was having to learn too much too fast, unassisted; I had nowhere to put it, no receptacle, pigeonhole prepared yet to accept it without pain and lacerations.
The Reivers by William Faulkner

Father said a man is the sum of his misfortunes. One day you'd think misfortune would get tired, but then time is your misfortune Father said.
The Sound and the Fury by William Faulkner

Earl (Bertrand Arthur William) Russell

Prize Motivation: "*The Nobel Prize in Literature 1950 was awarded to Bertrand Russell in recognition of his varied and significant writings in which he champions humanitarian ideals and freedom of thought.*"
Prize Year: *1950*
Prize Category: *Literature*
Source: nobelprize.org

In the tragic situation which confronts humanity, we feel that scientists should assemble in conference to appraise the perils that have arisen as a result of the development of weapons of mass destruction... There lies before us, if we choose, continual progress in happiness, knowledge, and wisdom. Shall we, instead, choose death, because we cannot forget our quarrels? We appeal, as human beings, to human beings: Remember your humanity, and forget the rest. If you can do so, the way lies open to a new Paradise; if you cannot, there lies before you the risk of universal death
The Russell-Einstein Manifesto, Issued in London, 9 July 1955

All definite knowledge—so I should contend—belongs to science; all dogma as to what surpasses definite knowledge belongs to theology. But between theology and science there is a No Man's Land, exposed to attack from both sides; this No Man's Land is philosophy.
History of Western Philosophy (Routledge Classics) by Bertrand Russell

When an intelligent man expresses a view which seems to us obviously absurd, we should not attempt to prove that it is somehow true, but we should try to understand how it ever came to seem true.
History of Western Philosophy (Routledge Classics) by Bertrand Russell

Much of what is greatest in human achievement involves some element of intoxication, some sweeping away of prudence by passion. Without the Bacchic element, life would be uninteresting; with it, it is dangerous. Prudence versus passion is a conflict that runs through history. It is not a conflict in which we ought to side wholly with either party.
History of Western Philosophy (Routledge Classics) by Bertrand Russell

Science tells us what we can know, but what we can know is little, and if we forget how much we cannot know we become insensitive to many things of very great importance. Theology, on the other hand, induces a dogmatic belief that we have knowledge where in fact we have ignorance, and by doing so generates a kind of impertinent insolence towards the universe. Uncertainty, in the presence of vivid hopes and fears, is painful, but must be endured if we wish to live without the support of comforting fairy tales.
History of Western Philosophy (Routledge Classics) by Bertrand Russell

So far as it lies in a man's own power, his life will realize its best possibilities if it has three things: creative rather than possessive impulses, reverence for others, and respect for the fundamental impulse in himself.
Political Ideals by Bertrand Russell

There can be no real freedom or democracy until the men who do the work in a business also control its management.
Political Ideals by Bertrand Russell

[A happy person] feels himself a citizen of the universe, enjoying freely the spectacle that it offers and the joy that it affords, untroubled by the thoughts of death because he feels himself not really separated from those who will come after him. It is in such a profound instinctive union with the stream of life that the greatest joy is to be found.
The Geography of Bliss: One Grump's Search for the Happiest Places in the World by Eric Weiner The Conquest of Happiness

Cruelty lurks in our instincts, and fanaticism is a camouflage for cruelty. Fanatics are seldom genuinely humane, and those who sincerely dread cruelty will be slow to adopt a fanatical creed.
The Practice and Theory of Bolshevism by Bertrand Russell

This seems plainly absurd; but whoever wishes to become a philosopher must learn not to be frightened by absurdities.
The Problems of Philosophy by Bertrand Russell

The idea that things must have a beginning is really due to the poverty of our imagination.
Why I am not a Christian: And Other Essays on Religion and Related Subjects by Bertrand Russell

Sir Winston Leonard Spencer Churchill

Prize Motivation: "*for his mastery of historical and biographical description as well as for brilliant oratory in defending exalted human values*"
Prize Year: *1953*
Prize Category: *Literature*
Source: nobelprize.org

Never give in — never, never, never, never, in nothing great or small, large or petty, never give in except to convictions of honour and good sense. Never yield to force; never yield to the apparently overwhelming might of the enemy.
Speech given at Harrow School, Harrow, England, October 29, 1941. Quoted in Churchill by Himself (2008), ed. Langworth, PublicAffairs, 2008, p. 23 ISBN 1586486381

The salvation of the common people of every race and of every land from war or servitudemust be established on solid foundations and must be guarded by the readiness of all men and women to die rather than submit to tyranny.
Speech at Zurich University (September 19, 1946) (partial text)

Success is the ability to go from one failure to another with no loss of enthusiasm.
1001 Smartest Things Ever Said by Steven D. Price

We live in a world of 'ifs.' 'What happened,' is singular; 'what might have happened,' legion.
4 Books By Sir Winston Churchill by Sir Winston S. Churchill

Although always prepared for martyrdom, I preferred that it should be postponed.
Bloodstone (A Reluctant Witch Mystery: Stacy Justice Book Two) by Barbra Annino My Early Life: A Roving Commission (1930) Sir Winston Churchill

There is no more delicious moment in the day than this, when we light the fire and, while the kettle boils, watch the dark shadows of the hills take form, perspective, and finally colour, knowing that there is another whole day begun, bright with chance and interest, and free from all cares.
London to Ladysmith via Pretoria by Sir Winston S. Churchill

If you are going through hell, keep going.
Sir Winston Churchill: His Wit and Wisdom by Jon Allen

All great movements, every vigorous impulse that a community may feel, become perverted and distorted as time passes, and the atmosphere of the earth seems fatal to the noble aspirations of its peoples. A wide humanitarian sympathy in a nation easily degenerates into hysteria. A military spirit tends towards brutality. Liberty leads to licence, restraint to tyranny. The pride of race is distended to blustering arrogance. The fear of God produces bigotry and superstition.

The River War: An Account of the Reconquest of the Sudan (mobi) by Sir Winston S. Churchill

It is a mistake to try to look too far ahead. The chain of destiny can only be grasped one link at a time.

Two Wars by Nate Self

It's not enough that we do our best; sometimes we have to do what's required.

Two Wars by Nate Self

Ernest Miller Hemingway

Prize Motivation: "*for his mastery of the art of narrative, most recently demonstrated in The Old Man and the Sea, and for the influence that he has exerted on contemporary style*"
Prize Year: *1954*
Prize Category: *Literature*
Source: <u>*nobelprize.org*</u>

If we win here we will win everywhere. The world is a fine place and worth the fighting for and I hate very much to leave it.
For Whom the Bell Tolls

Abstract words such as glory, honor, courage, or hallow were obscene beside the concrete names of villages, the numbers of roads, the names of rivers, the numbers of regiments and the dates.
A Farewell to Arms by Ernest Hemingway

I know that the night is not the same as the day: that all things are different, that the things of the night cannot be explained in the day, because they do not then exist, and the night can be a dreadful time for lonely people once their loneliness has started.
A Farewell to Arms by Ernest Hemingway

All you have to do is write one true sentence. Write the truest sentence that you know.
A Moveable Feast by Ernest Hemingway

I always worked until I had something done and I always stopped when I knew what was going to happen next. That way I could be sure of going on the next day.
A Moveable Feast by Ernest Hemingway

So far, about morals, I know only that what is moral is what you feel good after and what is immoral is what you feel bad after and judged by these moral standards, which I do not defend, the bullfight is very moral to me because I feel very fine while it is going on and have a feeling of life and death and mortality and immortality, and after it is over I feel very sad but very fine.
Death in the Afternoon by Ernest Hemingway

Madame, all stories, if continued far enough, end in death, and he is no true-story teller who would keep that from you. Especially do all stories of monogamy end in death, and your man who is monogamous while he often lives most happily, dies in the most lonely fashion. There is no lonelier man in death, except the suicide, than that man who has lived many years with a good wife and then outlived her. If two people love each other there can be no happy end to it.
Death in the Afternoon by Ernest Hemingway

To worry was as bad as to be afraid. It simply made things more difficult.
For Whom the Bell Tolls by Ernest Hemingway

Today is only one day in all the days that will ever be. But what will happen in all the other days that ever come can depend on what you do today.
For Whom the Bell Tolls by Ernest Hemingway

You have it now and that is all your whole life is; now. There is nothing else than now. There is neither yesterday, certainly, nor is there any tomorrow. How old must you be before you know that? There is only now, and if now is only two days, then two days is your life and everything in it will be in proportion. This is how you live a life in two days. And if you stop complaining and asking for what you never will get, you will have a good life. A good life is not measured by any biblical span.
For Whom the Bell Tolls by Ernest Hemingway

The way to hunt is for as long as you live against as long as there is such and such an animal; just as the way to paint is as long as there is you and colors and canvas, and to write as long as you can live and there is pencil and paper or ink or any machine to do it with, or anything you care to write about, and you feel a fool, and you are a fool, to do it any other way.
Green Hills of Africa by Ernest Hemingway

He did not want any consequences. He did not want any consequences ever again. He wanted to live along without consequences.
In Our Time by Ernest Hemingway

Out of all the things you could not have there were some that you could have and one of those was to know when you were happy and to enjoy all of it while it was there and it was good.
Islands in the Stream by Ernest Hemingway

You have to make it inside of yourself wherever you are. You are doing all right at that here.
Islands in the Stream by Ernest Hemingway

You see Eddy's happy because he does something well and does it every day."
Islands in the Stream by Ernest Hemingway

He had destroyed his talent by not using it, by betrayals of himself and what he believed in, by drinking so much that he blunted the edge of his perceptions, by laziness, by sloth, and by snobbery, by pride and by prejudice, by hook and by crook. What was this? A catalogue of old books? What was his talent anyway? It was a talent all right but instead of using it, he had traded on it. It was never what he had done, but always what he could do.
The Complete Short Stories Of Ernest Hemingway by Ernest Hemingway

They are, he thought, the hardest in the world; the hardest, the cruelest, the most predatory and the most attractive and their men have softened or gone to pieces nervously as they have hardened. Or is it that they pick men they can handle? They can't know that much at the age they marry, he thought. He was grateful that he had gone through his education on American women before now because this was a very attractive one.
The Complete Short Stories Of Ernest Hemingway by Ernest Hemingway

if she doesn't catch cold when she is rained on and appreciates dust, likes disorder and irregular meals and never needs to sleep and still keeps clean and neat without running water; then bring her. You'll probably lose her to a better man than you.
The Dangerous Summer by Ernest Hemingway

"Happiness in intelligent people is the rarest thing I know."
The Garden of Eden by Ernest Hemingway

Remember everything is right until it's wrong. You'll know when it's wrong.
The Garden of Eden by Ernest Hemingway

But man is not made for defeat, he said. A man can be destroyed but not defeated.
The Old Man and the Sea by Ernest Hemingway

You are killing me, fish, the old man thought. But you have a right to. Never have I seen a greater, or more beautiful, or a calmer or more noble thing than you, brother. Come on and kill me. I do not care who kills who.
The Old Man and the Sea by Ernest Hemingway

It is awfully easy to be hard-boiled about everything in the daytime, but at night it is another thing.
The Sun Also Rises by Ernest Hemingway

You can't get away from yourself by moving from one place to another. There's nothing to that.
The Sun Also Rises by Ernest Hemingway

Nobody ever lives their life all the way up except bull-fighters.
The Sun Also Rises by Ernest Hemingway

Enjoying living was learning to get your money's worth and knowing when you had it.
The Sun Also Rises by Ernest Hemingway

You're an expatriate. You've lost touch with the soil. You get precious. Fake European standards have ruined you. You drink yourself to death. You become obsessed by sex. You spend all your time talking, not working. You are an expatriate, see? You hang around cafés.
The Sun Also Rises by Ernest Hemingway

In Africa a thing is true at first light and a lie by noon and you have no more respect for it than for the lovely, perfect weed-fringed lake you see across the sun-baked salt plain. You have walked across that plain in the morning and you know that no such lake is there. But now it is there absolutely true, beautiful and believable.
True at First Light by Ernest Hemingway

Albert Camus

Prize Motivation: "*for his important literary production, which with clear-sighted earnestness illuminates the problems of the human conscience in our times*"
Prize Year: *1957*
Prize Category: *Literature*
Source: nobelprize.org

Each generation doubtless feels called upon to reform the world. Mine knows that it will not reform it, but its task is perhaps even greater. It consists in preventing the world from destroying itself. Heir to a corrupt history, in which are mingled fallen revolutions, technology gone mad, dead gods, and worn-out ideologies, where mediocre powers can destroy all yet no longer know how to convince, where intelligence has debased itself to become the servant of hatred and oppression, this generation starting from its own negations has had to re-establish, both within and without, a little of that which constitutes the dignity of life and death.
"Albert Camus - Banquet Speech". Nobelprize.org. 15 Nov 2012

The artist forges himself to the others, midway between the beauty he cannot do without and the community he cannot tear himself away from. That is why true artists scorn nothing: they are obliged to understand rather than to judge. And if they have to take sides in this world, they can perhaps side only with that society in which, according to Nietzsche's great words, not the judge but the creator will rule, whether he be a worker or an intellectual.
"Albert Camus - Banquet Speech". Nobelprize.org. 15 Nov 2012

Truth is mysterious, elusive, always to be conquered. Liberty is dangerous, as hard to live with as it is elating. We must march toward these two goals, painfully but resolutely, certain in advance of our failings on so long a road.
"Albert Camus - Banquet Speech". Nobelprize.org. 15 Nov 2012

But who can always sleep alone? Some men do, cut off from others by a vocation or misfortune, who go to bed every night in the same bed as death.
Exile and The Kingdom by Albert Camus

Since the beginning of time, on the dry earth of this limitless land scraped to the bone, a few men had been ceaselessly trudging, possessing nothing but serving no one, poverty-stricken but free lords of a strange kingdom.
Exile and The Kingdom by Albert Camus

Whoever gives nothing has nothing. The greatest misfortune is not to be unloved, but not to love.
Notebooks 1951-1959 by Albert Camus, Ryan Bloom, Ryan Bloom

Stupidity has a knack of getting its way; as we should see if we were not always so much wrapped up in ourselves.
The Plague Albert Camus

The evil that is in the world always comes of ignorance, and good intentions may do as much harm as malevolence, if they lack understanding. On the whole, men are more good than bad; that, however, isn't the real point. But they are more or less ignorant, and it is this that we call vice or virtue; the most incorrigible vice being that of an ignorance that fancies it knows everything and therefore claims for itself the right to kill. The soul of the murderer is blind; and there can be no true goodness nor true love without the utmost clear-sightedness.
The Plague Albert Camus

There have been as many plagues as wars in history; yet always plagues and wars take people equally by surprise.
The Plague Albert Camus

A pestilence isn't a thing made to man's measure; therefore we tell ourselves that pestilence is a mere bogy of the mind, a bad dream that will pass away. But it doesn't always pass away and, from one bad dream to another, it is men who pass away, and the humanists first of all, because they haven't taken their precautions.
The Plague Albert Camus

Query: How contrive not to waste one's time? Answer: By being fully aware of it all the while. Ways in which this can be done: By spending one's days on an uneasy chair in a dentist's waiting-room; by remaining on one's balcony all a Sunday afternoon; by listening to lectures in a language one doesn't know; by traveling by the longest and least-convenient train routes, and of course standing all the way; by lining up at the box-office of theaters and then not buying a seat; and so forth.
The Plague Albert Camus

John Steinbeck

Prize Motivation: "*for his realistic and imaginative writings, combining as they do sympathetic humour and keen social perception*"
Prize Year: *1962*
Prize Category: *Literature*
Source: nobelprize.org

The ancient commission of the writer has not changed. He is charged with exposing our many grievous faults and failures, with dredging up to the light our dark and dangerous dreams for the purpose of improvement.
"John Steinbeck - Banquet Speech". Nobelprize.org. 17 Nov 2012

Literature is as old as speech. It grew out of human need for it, and it has not changed except to become more needed.
"John Steinbeck - Banquet Speech". Nobelprize.org. 17 Nov 2012

We have usurped many of the powers we once ascribed to God. Fearful and unprepared, we have assumed lordship over the life or death of the whole world - of all living things. The danger and the glory and the choice rest finally in man. The test of his perfectibility is at hand. Having taken Godlike power, we must seek in ourselves for the responsibility and the wisdom we once prayed some deity might have. Man himself has become our greatest hazard and our only hope.
"John Steinbeck - Banquet Speech". Nobelprize.org. 17 Nov 2012

He can kill anything for need but he could not even hurt a feeling for pleasure.
Cannery Row by John Steinbeck

Someone should write an erudite essay on the moral, physical, and esthetic effect of the Model T Ford on the American nation. Two generations of Americans knew more about the Ford coil than the clitoris, about the planetary system of gears than the solar system of stars.
Cannery Row by John Steinbeck

And this I believe: that the free, exploring mind of the individual human is the most valuable thing in the world. And this I would fight for: the freedom of the mind to take any direction it wishes, undirected. And this I must fight against: any idea, religion, or government which limits or destroys the individual.
East of Eden by John Steinbeck

We have only one story. All novels, all poetry, are built on the never-ending contest in ourselves of good and evil. And it occurs to me that evil must constantly respawn, while good, while virtue, is immortal. Vice has always a new fresh young face, while virtue is venerable as nothing else in the world is.
East of Eden by John Steinbeck

As happens sometimes, a moment settled and hovered and remained for much more than a moment. And sound stopped and movement stopped for much, much more than a moment.
Of Mice and Men by John Steinbeck

For the quality of owning freezes you forever into "I," and cuts you off forever from the "we."
The Grapes of Wrath by John Steinbeck

How can we live without our lives? How will we know it's us without our past?
The Grapes of Wrath by John Steinbeck

A man who tells secrets or stories must think of who is hearing or reading, for a story has as many versions as it has readers. Everyone takes what he wants or can from it and thus changes it to his measure. Some pick out parts and reject the rest, some strain the story through their mesh of prejudice, some paint it with their own delight. A story must have some points of contact with the reader to make him feel at home in it. Only then can he accept wonders.
The Winter of Our Discontent by John Steinbeck

And if I should put the rules aside for a time, I knew I would wear scars but would they be worse than the scars of failure I was wearing? To be alive at all is to have scars.
The Winter of Our Discontent by John Steinbeck

So many old and lovely things are stored in the world's attic, because we don't want them around us and we don't dare throw them out.
The Winter of Our Discontent by John Steinbeck

Tom Wolfe was right. You can't go home again because home has ceased to exist except in the mothballs of memory.
Travels with Charley in Search of America by John Steinbeck

When people are engaged in something they are not proud of, they do not welcome witnesses. In fact, they come to believe the witness causes the trouble.
Travels with Charley in Search of America by John Steinbeck

Aleksandr Isayevich Solzhenitsyn

 **Prize Motivation:** "*for the ethical force with which he has pursued the indispensable traditions of Russian literature*"
Prize Year: *1970*
Prize Category: *Literature*
Source: nobelprize.org

But now during the past few decades, imperceptibly, suddenly, mankind has become one - hopefully one and dangerously one - so that the concussions and inflammations of one of its parts are almost instantaneously passed on to others, sometimes lacking in any kind of necessary immunity. Mankind has become one, but not steadfastly one as communities or even nations used to be; not united through years of mutual experience, neither through possession of a single eye, affectionately called crooked, nor yet through a common native language, but, surpassing all barriers, through international broadcasting and print.
"Alexandr Solzhenitsyn - Nobel Lecture". Nobelprize.org. 20 Nov 2012

But a work of art bears within itself its own verification: conceptions which are devised or stretched do not stand being portrayed in images, they all come crashing down, appear sickly and pale, convince no one. But those works of art which have scooped up the truth and presented it to us as a living force - they take hold of us, compel us, and nobody ever, not even in ages to come, will appear to refute them.
"Alexandr Solzhenitsyn - Nobel Lecture". Nobelprize.org. 20 Nov 2012

One day Dostoevsky threw out the enigmatic remark: "Beauty will save the world". What sort of a statement is that? For a long time I considered it mere words. How could that be possible? When in bloodthirsty history did beauty ever save anyone from anything? Ennobled, uplifted, yes - but whom has it saved? There is, however, a certain peculiarity in the essence of beauty, a peculiarity in the status of art: namely, the convincingness of a true work of art is completely irrefutable and it forces even an opposing heart to surrender.
"Alexandr Solzhenitsyn - Nobel Lecture". Nobelprize.org. 20 Nov 2012

And obviously she was right. It is not our level of prosperity that makes for happiness but the kinship of heart to heart and the way we look at the world. Both attitudes lie within our power, so that a man is happy so long as he chooses to be happy, and no one can stop him.
Cancer Ward by Aleksandr Solzhenitsyn

The meaning of existence was to preserve untarnished, undisturbed and undistorted the image of eternity which each person is born with – as far as is possible. Like a silver moon in a calm, still pond.
Cancer Ward by Aleksandr Solzhenitsyn

If only it were all so simple! If only there were evil people somewhere insidiously committing evil deeds, and it were necessary only to separate them from the rest of us and destroy them. But the line dividing good and evil cuts through the heart of every human being. And who is willing to destroy a piece of his own heart?
The Gulag Archipelago by Aleksandr Solzhenitsyn

Ideology—that is what gives evildoing its long-sought justification and gives the evildoer the necessary steadfastness and determination.
The Gulag Archipelago by Aleksandr Solzhenitsyn

Each of us is a center of the Universe, and that Universe is shattered when they hiss at you: "You are under arrest."
The Gulag Archipelago by Aleksandr Solzhenitsyn

Own only what you can always carry with you: know languages, know countries, know people. Let your memory be your travel bag. Use your memory! Use your memory! It is those bitter seeds alone which might sprout and grow someday.
The Gulag Archipelago by Aleksandr Solzhenitsyn

A person who is not inwardly prepared for the use of violence against him is always weaker than the person committing the violence.
The Gulag Archipelago, 1918-1956: An Experiment in Literary Investigation (Volume One): 001 by Aleksandr I. Solzhenitsyn

Toni Morrison

Prize Motivation: "*who in novels characterized by visionary force and poetic import, gives life to an essential aspect of American reality*"
Prize Year: *1993*
Prize Category: *Literature*
Source: nobelprize.org

Anger... it's a paralyzing emotion... you can't get anything done. People sort of think it's an interesting, passionate, and igniting feeling — I don't think it's any of that — it's helpless... it's absence of control — and I need all of my skills, all of the control, all of my powers — and I need clarity, in order to write — and anger doesn't provide any of that — I have no use for it whatsoever. I can feel melancholy, and I can feel full of regret, but anger is something that is useful to the people who watch it... it's not useful to me.
Interview with Don Swaim (1987)

At some point in life the world's beauty becomes enough. You don't need to photograph, paint or even remember it. It is enough. No record of it needs to be kept and you don't need someone to share it with or tell it to. When that happens — that letting go — you let go because you can.
Tar Baby (1981)

It was not a miracle. Bestowed by God. It was a mercy. Offered by a human. I stayed on my knees. In the dust where my heart will remain each night and every day until you understand what I know and long to tell you: to be given dominion over another is a hard thing; to wrest dominion over another is a wrong thing; to give dominion of yourself to another is a wicked thing.
A Mercy by Toni Morrison

Freeing yourself was one thing; claiming ownership of that freed self was another.
Beloved by Toni Morrison

She told them that the only grace they could have was the grace they could imagine. That if they could not see it, they would not have it.
Beloved by Toni Morrison

...to get to a place where you could love anything you chose—not to need permission for desire—well now, that was freedom.
Beloved by Toni Morrison

"She is a friend of my mind. She gather me, man. The pieces I am, she gather them and give them back to me in all the right order. It's good, you know, when you got a woman who is a friend of your mind."
Beloved by Toni Morrison

Nowadays silence is looked on as odd and most of my race has forgotten the beauty of meaning much by saying little.
Love by Toni Morrison

Hate does that. Burns off everything but itself, so whatever your grievance is, your face looks just like your enemy's.
Love (Morrison, Toni) by Toni Morrison

Love is divine only and difficult always. If you think it is easy you are a fool. If you think it is natural you are blind. It is a learned application without reason or motive except that it is God.
Paradise by Toni Morrison

Love is not a gift. It is a diploma. A diploma conferring certain privileges: the privilege of expressing love and the privilege of receiving it.
Paradise by Toni Morrison

Let me tell you right now the one important thing you'll ever need to know: Own things. And let the things you own own other things. Then you'll own yourself and other people too.
Song of Solomon by Toni Morrison

You think dark is just one color, but it ain't. There're five or six kinds of black. Some silky, some woolly. Some just empty. Some like fingers. And it don't stay still. It moves and changes from one kind of black to another. Saying something is pitch black is like saying something is green.
Song of Solomon by Toni Morrison

A daughter is a woman that cares about where she come from and takes care of them that took care of her.
Tar Baby by Toni Morrison

Love is never any better than the lover. Wicked people love wickedly, violent people love violently, weak people love weakly, stupid people love stupidly, but the love of a free man is never safe.
The Bluest Eye by Toni Morrison

Misery colored by the greens and blues in my mother's voice took all of the grief out of the words and left me with a conviction that pain was not only endurable, it was sweet.
The Bluest Eye (Vintage International) by Toni Morrison

Along with the idea of romantic love, she was introduced to another—physical beauty. Probably the most destructive ideas in the history of human thought. Both originated in envy, thrived in insecurity, and ended in disillusion. In equating physical beauty with virtue, she stripped her mind, bound it, and collected self-contempt by the heap. She forgot lust and simple caring for.

The Bluest Eye (Vintage International) by Toni Morrison

Sir Vidiadhar Surajprasad Naipaul

Prize Motivation: "*for having united perceptive narrative and incorruptible scrutiny in works that compel us to see the presence of suppressed histories*"
Prize Year: *2001*
Prize Category: *Literature*
Source: *nobelprize.org*

Most people are not really free. They are confined by the niche in the world that they carve out for themselves. They limit themselves to fewer possibilities by the narrowness of their vision.

Life doesn't have a neat beginning and a tidy end, life is always going on. You should begin in the middle and end in the middle, and it should be all there.
Half a Life (2001)

Everybody is interesting for an hour, but few people can last more than two.
Quoted in "Wanderer of Endless Curiosity" by R. Z. Sheppard in Time magazine (10 July 1989)

One isn't born one's self. One is born with a mass of expectations, a mass of other people's ideas — and you have to work through it all.
Quoted in "V.S. Naipaul in Search of Himself: A Conversation" with Mel Gussow, The New York Times, (24 April 1994)

The world is what it is; men who are nothing, who allow themselves to become nothing, have no place in it.
A Bend in the River by V.S. Naipaul

And this is where I suppose life ends for most people, who stiffen in the attitudes they adopt to make themselves suitable for the jobs and lives that other people have laid out for them.
A Bend in the River by V.S. Naipaul

After all, we make ourselves according to the ideas we have of our possibilities.
A Bend in the River by V.S. Naipaul

Non-fiction can distort; facts can be realigned. But fiction never lies.
A Bend in the River by V.S. Naipaul

V. S. Naipaul once said, "The politics of a country can only be an extension of its human relationships."
Imagining India: The Idea of a Renewed Nation by Nandan Nilekani

It is wrong to have an ideal view of the world. That's where the mischief starts. That's where everything starts unravelling.
Magic Seeds by V.S. Naipaul

Peace Nobel Laureates

Theodore Roosevelt

Prize Motivation: "*The Nobel Peace Prize 1906 was awarded to Theodore Roosevelt.*"
Prize Year: *1906*
Prize Category: *Peace*
Source: *nobelprize.org*

The first essential of civilization is law. Anarchy is simply the handmaiden and forerunner of tyranny and despotism. Law and order enforced with justice and by strength lie at the foundations of civilization. Law must be based upon justice, else it cannot stand, and it must be enforced with resolute firmness, because weakness in enforcing it means in the end that there is no justice and no law, nothing but the rule of disorderly and unscrupulous strength. Without the habit of orderly obedience to the law, without the stern enforcement of the laws at the expense of those who defiantly resist them, there can be no possible progress, moral or material, in civilization.
National Duties

Address at the Minnesota State Fair, St. Paul, 2 September 1901

Our words must be judged by our deeds; and in striving for a lofty ideal we must use practical methods; and if we cannot attain all at one leap, we must advance towards it step by step, reasonably content so long as we do actually make some progress in the right direction.
"Theodore Roosevelt - Acceptance Speech". Nobelprize.org. 15 Nov 2012

Death is always and under all circumstances a tragedy, for if it is not, then it means that life itself has become one.
Letter to Cecil Spring-Rice (12 March 1900).

I have always been fond of the West African proverb "Speak softly and carry a big stick; you will go far."
Letter to Henry L. Sprague (26 January 1900); this is the first known use of this phrase, which became a signature motto of Roosevelt's after he used it in a speech as Vice-President at the Minnesota State Fair:

"Take care of your morals first, your health next, and finally your studies."
The Rise of Theodore Roosevelt (Modern Library Paperbacks) by Edmund Morris

it is the availability of raw power, not the use of it, that makes for effective diplomacy.
The Rise of Theodore Roosevelt (Modern Library Paperbacks) by Edmund Morris

"If a man has a very decided character, has a strongly accentuated career, it is normally the case of course that he makes ardent friends and bitter enemies."
The Rise of Theodore Roosevelt (Modern Library Paperbacks) by Edmund Morris

"A just war is in the long run far better for a man's soul than the most prosperous peace."
The Rise of Theodore Roosevelt (Modern Library Paperbacks) by Edmund Morris

"I love peace, but it is because I love justice and not because I am afraid of war,"
The River of Doubt: Theodore Roosevelt's Darkest Journey by Candice Millard

Credit should go with the performance of duty, and not with what is very often the accident of glory.
The Rough Riders by Theodore Roosevelt

Jane Addams

Prize Motivation: "*The Nobel Peace Prize 1931 was awarded jointly to Jane Addams and Nicholas Murray Butler*"
Prize Year: *1931*
Prize Category: *Peace*
Source: nobelprize.org

To attain individual morality in an age demanding social morality, to pride one's self on the results of personal effort when the time demands social adjustment, is utterly to fail to apprehend the situation.
Democracy and Social Ethics by Jane Addams

We are thus brought to a conception of Democracy not merely as a sentiment which desires the well-being of all men, nor yet as a creed which believes in the essential dignity and equality of all men, but as that which affords a rule of living as well as a test of faith.
Democracy and Social Ethics by Jane Addams

We know instinctively that if we grow contemptuous of our fellows, and consciously limit our intercourse to certain kinds of people whom we have previously decided to respect, we not only tremendously circumscribe our range of life, but limit the scope of our ethics.
Democracy and Social Ethics by Jane Addams

Formerly when it was believed that poverty was synonymous with vice and laziness, and that the prosperous man was the righteous man, charity was administered harshly with a good conscience; for the charitable agent really blamed the individual for his poverty, and the very fact of his own superior prosperity gave him a certain consciousness of superior morality.
Democracy and Social Ethics by Jane Addams

It is perhaps significant that a German critic has of late reminded us that the one test which the most authoritative and dramatic portrayal of the Day of Judgment offers, is the social test. The stern questions are not in regard to personal and family relations, but did ye visit the poor, the criminal, the sick, and did ye feed the hungry?
Democracy and Social Ethics by Jane Addams

We slowly learn that life consists of processes as well as results, and that failure may come quite as easily from ignoring the adequacy of one's method as from selfish or ignoble aims.
Democracy and Social Ethics by Jane Addams

It is well to remind ourselves, from time to time, that "Ethics" is but another word for "righteousness," that for which many men and women of every generation have hungered and thirsted, and without which life becomes meaningless.
Democracy and Social Ethics by Jane Addams

If you think for yourself in choosing your hopes and then are realistic about what it will take to achieve them, you will release your own spirit into action with wonderfully useful results.
Jane Addams: Spirit in Action by Louise W. Knight

it was very important not to pretend to understand what you didn't understand and that you must always be honest with yourself inside, whatever happened.
Twenty Years at Hull House; with autobiographical notes by Jane Addams

Those who believe that Justice is but a poetical longing within us, the enthusiast who thinks it will come in the form of a millennium, those who see it established by the strong arm of a hero, are not those who have comprehended the vast truths of life. The actual Justice must come by trained intelligence, by broadened sympathies toward the individual man or woman who crosses our path; one item added to another is the only method by which to build up a conception lofty enough to be of use in the world.
Twenty Years at Hull House; with autobiographical notes by Jane Addams

Martin Luther King Jr.

Prize Motivation: "*The Nobel Peace Prize 1964 was awarded to Martin Luther King Jr..*"
Prize Year: *1964*
Prize Category: *Peace*
Source: nobelprize.org

But in spite of temporary victories, violence never brings permanent peace. It solves no social problem: it merely creates new and more complicated ones. Violence is impractical because it is a descending spiral ending in destruction for all. It is immoral because it seeks to humiliate the opponent rather than win his understanding: it seeks to annihilate rather than convert. Violence is immoral because it thrives on hatred rather than love. It destroys community and makes brotherhood impossible. It leaves society in monologue rather than dialogue. Violence ends up defeating itself. It creates bitterness in the survivors and brutality in the destroyers.
"Martin Luther King Jr. - Nobel Lecture Speech". Nobelprize.org. 26 Nov 2012

We will not build a peaceful world by following a negative path. It is not enough to say "We must not wage war." It is necessary to love peace and sacrifice for it. We must concentrate not merely on the negative expulsion of war, but on the positive affirmation of peace.
"Martin Luther King Jr. - Nobel Lecture Speech". Nobelprize.org. 26 Nov 2012

I believe that wounded justice, lying prostrate on the blood-flowing streets of our nations, can be lifted from this dust of shame to reign supreme among the children of men. I have the audacity to believe that peoples everywhere can have three meals a day for their bodies, education and culture for their minds, and dignity, equality and freedom for their spirits. I believe that what self-centered men have torn down men other-centered can build up. I still believe that one day mankind will bow before the altars of God and be crowned triumphant over war and bloodshed, and nonviolent redemptive good will proclaim the rule of the land. "And the lion and the lamb shall lie down together and every man shall sit under his own vine and fig tree and none shall be afraid." I still believe that We Shall overcome!
"Martin Luther King Jr. - Acceptance Speech". Nobelprize.org. 26 Nov 2012

...the beauty of genuine brotherhood and peace is more precious than diamonds or silver or gold.
"Martin Luther King Jr. - Acceptance Speech". Nobelprize.org. 26 Nov 2012

When our days become dreary with low-hovering clouds and our nights become darker than a thousand midnights, we will know that we are living in the creative turmoil of a genuine civilization struggling to be born.
"Martin Luther King Jr. - Acceptance Speech". Nobelprize.org. 26 Nov 2012

I refuse to accept despair as the final response to the ambiguities of history. I refuse to accept the idea that the "isness" of man's present nature makes him morally incapable of reaching up for the eternal "oughtness" that forever confronts him. I refuse to accept the idea that man is mere flotsam and jetsam in the river of life, unable to influence the unfolding events which surround him. I refuse to accept the view that mankind is so tragically bound to the starless midnight of racism and war that the bright daybreak of peace and brotherhood can never become a reality. I refuse to accept the cynical notion that nation after nation must spiral down a militaristic stairway into the hell of thermonuclear destruction. I believe that unarmed truth and unconditional love will have the final word in reality. This is why right, temporarily defeated, is stronger than evil triumphant.
"Martin Luther King Jr. - Acceptance Speech". Nobelprize.org. 26 Nov 2012

Nonviolence is the answer to the crucial political and moral questions of our time — the need for mankind to overcome oppression and violence without resorting to violence and oppression. Civilization and violence are antithetical concepts… Sooner or later all the people of the world will have to discover a way to live together in peace, and thereby transform this pending cosmic elegy into a creative psalm of brotherhood. If this is to be achieved, man must evolve for all human conflict a method which rejects revenge, aggression and retaliation. The foundation of such a method is love.
"Martin Luther King Jr. - Acceptance Speech". Nobelprize.org. 26 Nov 2012

It really boils down to this: that all life is interrelated. We are all caught in an inescapable network of mutuality, tied into a single garment of destiny. Whatever affects one directly, affects all indirectly.
The Trumpet of Conscience (King Legacy) by Martin Luther King Jr.

A social movement that only moves people is merely a revolt. A movement that changes both people and institutions is a revolution.
Why We Can't Wait (King Legacy) by Martin Luther King Jr.

"Punish me. I do not deserve it. But because I do not deserve it, I will accept it so that the world will know that I am right and you are wrong," you hardly know what to do. You feel defeated and secretly ashamed. You know that this man is as good a man as you are; that from some mysterious source he has found the courage and the conviction to meet physical force with soul force.
Why We Can't Wait (King Legacy) by Martin Luther King Jr.

The Negro turned his back on force not only because he knew he could not win his freedom through physical force but also because he believed that through physical force he could lose his soul.
Why We Can't Wait (King Legacy) by Martin Luther King Jr.

Henry A. Kissinger

Prize Motivation: "*The Nobel Peace Prize 1973 was awarded jointly to Henry A. Kissinger and Le Duc Tho*"
Prize Year: *1973*
Prize Category: *Peace*
Source: *nobelprize.org*

America's goal is the building of a structure of peace, a peace in which all nations have a stake and therefore to which all nations have a commitment. We are seeking a stable world, not as an end in itself but as a bridge to the realisation of man's noble aspirations of tranquility and community.
"Henry Kissinger - Acceptance Speech". Nobelprize.org. 15 Nov 2012

To the realist, peace represents a stable arrangement of power; to the idealist, a goal so pre-eminent that it conceals the difficulty of finding the means to its achievement. But in this age of thermonuclear technology, neither view can assure man's preservation. Instead, peace, the ideal, must be practised. A sense of responsibility and accommodation must guide the behavior of all nations. Some common notion of justice can and must be found, for failure to do so will only bring more "just" wars.
"Henry Kissinger - Acceptance Speech". Nobelprize.org. 15 Nov 2012

Our experience has taught us to regard peace as a delicate, ever-fleeting condition, its roots too shallow to bear the strain of social and political discontent. We tend to accept the lessons of that experience and work toward those solutions that at best relieve specific sources of strain, lest our neglect allows war to overtake peace.
"Henry Kissinger - Acceptance Speech". Nobelprize.org. 15 Nov 2012

The purpose of the separation of powers was to avoid despotism, not to achieve harmonious government;
Diplomacy (A Touchstone book) by Henry Kissinger

Empires have no interest in operating within an international system; they aspire to be the international system. Empires have no need for a balance of power. That is how the United States has conducted its foreign policy in the Americas, and China through most of its history in Asia.
Diplomacy (A Touchstone book) by Henry Kissinger

What is new about the emerging world order is that, for the first time, the United States can neither withdraw from the world nor dominate it.
Diplomacy (A Touchstone book) by Henry Kissinger

The balance of power reduces the opportunities for using force; a shared sense of justice reduces the desire to use force.
Diplomacy (A Touchstone book) by Henry Kissinger

A turbulent history has taught Chinese leaders that not every problem has a solution and that too great an emphasis on total mastery over specific events could upset the harmony of the universe.
On China by Henry Kissinger

What distinguishes Sun Tzu from Western writers on strategy is the emphasis on the psychological and political elements over the purely military.
On China by Henry Kissinger

Where the Western tradition prized the decisive clash of forces emphasizing feats of heroism, the Chinese ideal stressed subtlety, indirection, and the patient accumulation of relative advantage.
On China by Henry Kissinger

Almost all empires were created by force, but none can be sustained by it. Universal rule, to last, needs to translate force into obligation. Otherwise, the energies of the rulers will be exhausted in maintaining their dominance at the expense of their ability to shape the future, which is the ultimate task of statesmanship. Empires persist if repression gives way to consensus.
On China by Henry Kissinger

Mother Teresa

Prize Motivation: "*The Nobel Peace Prize 1979 was awarded to Mother Teresa.*"
Prize Year: *1979*
Prize Category: *Peace*
Source: *nobelprize.org*

Love has no meaning if it isn't shared. Love has to be put into action. You have to love without expectation, to do something for love itself, not for what you may receive. If you expect something in return, then it isn't love, because true love is loving without conditions and expectations.
A Simple Path: 1 by Mother Teresa

Don't look for big things, just do small things with great love… The smaller the thing, the greater must be our love.
Mother Teresa: Come Be My Light by Mother Teresa, Brian Kolodiejchuk

Take whatever He gives and give whatever He takes with a big smile.
Mother Teresa: Come Be My Light by Mother Teresa, Brian Kolodiejchuk

If you are discouraged, it is a sign of pride because it shows you trust in your own powers. Never bother about people's opinions. Be humble and you will never be disturbed. The Lord has willed me here where I am. He will offer a solution.
No Greater Love by Mother Teresa

It does not matter how much we give, but how much love we put into our giving.
No Greater Love by Mother Teresa

True love is love that causes us pain, that hurts, and yet brings us joy. That is why we must pray to God and ask Him to give us the courage to love.
No Greater Love by Mother Teresa

You learn humility only by accepting humiliations. And you will meet humiliation all through your life. The greatest humiliation is to know that you are nothing. This you come to know when you face God in prayer.
No Greater Love by Mother Teresa

At the moment of death, we will not be judged by the amount of work we have done but by the weight of love we have put into our work. This love should flow from self-sacrifice, and it must be felt to the point of hurting.
No Greater Love by Mother Teresa

What we need is to love without getting tired. How does a lamp burn? Through the continuous input of small drops of oil. What are these drops of oil in our lamps? They are the small things of daily life: faithfulness, small words of kindness, a thought for others, our way of being silent, of looking, of speaking, and of acting. Do not look for Jesus away from yourselves. He is not out there; He is in you. Keep your lamp burning, and you will recognize Him.

No Greater Love by Mother Teresa

Let no one ever come to you without leaving better and happier. Be the living expression of God's kindness: kindness in your face, kindness in your eyes, kindness in your smile.

The Heart of Abundance: A Simple Guide to Appreciating and Enjoying Life by Candy Paull

Elie Wiesel

Prize Motivation: "*The Nobel Peace Prize 1986 was awarded to Elie Wiesel.*"
Prize Year: *1986*
Prize Category: *Peace*
Source: nobelprize.org

No one is as capable of gratitude as one who has emerged from the kingdom of night. We know that every moment is a moment of grace, every hour an offering; not to share them would mean to betray them. Our lives no longer belong to us alone; they belong to all those who need us desperately.
"Elie Wiesel - Acceptance Speech". Nobelprize.org. 15 Nov 2012

As long as one dissident is in prison, our freedom will not be true. As long as one child is hungry, our lives will be filled with anguish and shame. What all these victims need above all is to know that they are not alone; that we are not forgetting them, that when their voices are stifled we shall lend them ours, that while their freedom depends on ours, the quality of our freedom depends on theirs.
"Elie Wiesel - Acceptance Speech". Nobelprize.org. 15 Nov 2012

Just as man cannot live without dreams, he cannot live without hope. If dreams reflect the past, hope summons the future. Does this mean that our future can be built on a rejection of the past? Surely such a choice is not necessary. The two are not incompatible. The opposite of the past is not the future but the absence of future; the opposite of the future is not the past but the absence of past. The loss of one is equivalent to the sacrifice of the other.
"Elie Wiesel - Acceptance Speech". Nobelprize.org. 15 Nov 2012

We must always take sides. Neutrality helps the oppressor, never the victim. Silence encourages the tormentor, never the tormented. Sometimes we must interfere. When human lives are endangered, when human dignity is in jeopardy, national borders and sensitivities become irrelevant. Wherever men or women are persecuted because of their race, religion, or political views, that place must – at that moment – become the center of the universe.
"Elie Wiesel - Acceptance Speech". Nobelprize.org. 15 Nov 2012

Without memory, our existence would be barren and opaque, like a prison cell into which no light penetrates; like a tomb which rejects the living.
"Elie Wiesel - Nobel Lecture: Hope, Despair and Memory". Nobelprize.org. 18 Nov 2012

"Sanctuary," Elie Wiesel says, "is often something very small. Not a grandiose gesture, but a small gesture toward alleviating human suffering and preventing humiliation. Sanctuary is a human being. Sanctuary is a dream. That is why you are here and that is why I am here; we are here because of one another. We are in truth each other's shelter."
A House for Hope: The Promise of Progressive Religion for the Twenty-First Century by Rebecca Ann Parker, John Buehrens

Love can degenerate into obsession, but friendship never means anything but sharing. It is with friends that we share the awakening of desire, the birth of a vision or a fear.
All Rivers Run to the Sea: Memoirs by Elie Wiesel

To write is to plumb the unfathomable depths of being. Writing lies within the domain of mystery. The space between any two words is vaster than the distance between heaven and earth. To bridge it you must close your eyes and leap. A Hasidic tradition tells us that in the Torah the white spaces, too, are God-given. Ultimately, to write is an act of faith.
All Rivers Run to the Sea: Memoirs by Elie Wiesel

Friendship or death, the Talmud says. Without friends, existence is empty, sterile, pointless. Friendship is even more important in a man's life than love. Love may drive one to kill, friendship never.
All Rivers Run to the Sea: Memoirs by Elie Wiesel

The danger lies in oblivion. Were I to forget where I come from, my life would become barren and sterile. Were I to forget whom I am the descendant of, I would be doomed to despair.
Rashi (Jewish Encounters) by Elie Wiesel

There is only one path known to a human being who lives in time: to live in the present using up all his resources, all his resilience. To make each day a source of grace, each hour an accomplishment, each wink of the eye an invitation to friendship. Each smile a promise. So long as the curtain has not fallen, everything remains possible.
The Sonderberg Case by Elie Wiesel

How can we act so that the tears of joy of one don't cause the anguished sobs of another? So that the hope of one isn't based on the despair of another?
The Sonderberg Case by Elie Wiesel

The moment we identify the genesis of a decision, we ought to be satisfied. And all the rest is commentary.
Wise Men and Their Tales: Portraits of Biblical, Talmudic, and Hasidic Masters by Elie Wiesel

Nelson Mandela

Prize Motivation: "*for their work for the peaceful termination of the apartheid regime, and for laying the foundations for a new democratic South Africa*"
Prize Year: *1993*
Prize Category: *Peace*
Source: *nobelprize.org*

The greatest glory in living lies not in never falling, but in rising every time we fall.
Long Walk to Freedom: The Autobiography of Nelson Mandela

I always remember the regent's axiom: a leader, he said, is like a shepherd. He stays behind the flock, letting the most nimble go out ahead, whereupon the others follow, not realizing that all along they are being directed from behind.
Long Walk to Freedom: The Autobiography of Nelson Mandela by Nelson Mandela

It is what we make out of what we have, not what we are given, that separates one person from another.
Long Walk to Freedom: The Autobiography of Nelson Mandela by Nelson Mandela

I learned that to humiliate another person is to make him suffer an unnecessarily cruel fate. Even as a boy, I defeated my opponents without dishonoring them.
Long Walk to Freedom: The Autobiography of Nelson Mandela by Nelson Mandela

There is nothing like returning to a place that remains unchanged to find the ways in which you yourself have altered.
Long Walk to Freedom: The Autobiography of Nelson Mandela by Nelson Mandela

A freedom fighter learns the hard way that it is the oppressor who defines the nature of the struggle, and the oppressed is often left no recourse but to use methods that mirror those of the oppressor. At a certain point, one can only fight fire with fire.
Long Walk to Freedom: The Autobiography of Nelson Mandela by Nelson Mandela

Without language, one cannot talk to people and understand them; one cannot share their hopes and aspirations, grasp their history, appreciate their poetry, or savor their songs. I again realized that we were not different people with separate languages; we were one people, with different tongues.
Long Walk to Freedom: The Autobiography of Nelson Mandela by Nelson Mandela

There is little favorable to be said about poverty, but it was often an incubator of true friendship. Many people will appear to befriend you when you are wealthy, but precious few will do the same when you are poor. If wealth is a magnet, poverty is a kind of repellent. Yet, poverty often brings out the true generosity in others.

Long Walk to Freedom: The Autobiography of Nelson Mandela by Nelson Mandela

I learned that courage was not the absence of fear, but the triumph over it. I felt fear myself more times than I can remember, but I hid it behind a mask of boldness. The brave man is not he who does not feel afraid, but he who conquers that fear.

Long Walk to Freedom: The Autobiography of Nelson Mandela by Nelson Mandela

There are times when a leader must move out ahead of the flock, go off in a new direction, confident that he is leading his people the right way.

Long Walk to Freedom: The Autobiography of Nelson Mandela by Nelson Mandela

Jimmy Carter

Prize Motivation: "*for his decades of untiring effort to find peaceful solutions to international conflicts, to advance democracy and human rights, and to promote economic and social development*"
Prize Year: *2002*
Prize Category: *Peace*
Source: nobelprize.org

The most serious and universal problem is the growing chasm between the richest and poorest people on earth. Citizens of the ten wealthiest countries are now seventy-five times richer than those who live in the ten poorest ones, and the separation is increasing every year, not only between nations but also within them.
"Jimmy Carter - Nobel Lecture". Nobelprize.org. 18 Nov 2012

Let us learn together and laugh together and work together and pray together, confident that in the end we will triumph together in the right.
Jimmy Carter Inaugural Address, 20 January 1977

Aggression unopposed becomes a contagious disease.
Quoted in "US-Pakistan Relationship: Soviet Invasion Of Afghanistan" - Page 73 - by A. Z. Hilali - Political Science - 2005

Despite theological differences, all great religions share common commitments that define our ideal secular relationships. I am convinced that Christians, Muslims, Buddhists, Hindus, Jews, and others can embrace each other in a common effort to alleviate human suffering and to espouse peace.
"Jimmy Carter - Nobel Lecture". Nobelprize.org. 18 Nov 2012

War may sometimes be a necessary evil. But no matter how necessary, it is always an evil, never a good. We will not learn how to live together in peace by killing each other's children. The bond of our common humanity is stronger than the divisiveness of our fears and prejudices. God gives us the capacity for choice. We can choose to alleviate suffering. We can choose to work together for peace. We can make these changes - and we must.

"Jimmy Carter - Nobel Lecture". Nobelprize.org. 18 Nov 2012

I believe that anyone can be successful in life, regardless of natural talent or the environment within which we live. This is not based on measuring success by human competitiveness for wealth, possessions, influence, and fame, but adhering to God's standards of truth, justice, humility, service, compassion, forgiveness, and love.
Our Endangered Values by Jimmy Carter

You only need two loves in your life: for God, and for the person in front of you at any particular time.
Our Endangered Values by Jimmy Carter

In the most recent year for which data are available, handguns killed 334 people in Australia, 197 in Great Britain, 183 in Sweden, 83 in Japan, 54 in Ireland, 1,034 in Canada, and 30,419 in the United States.
Our Endangered Values by Jimmy Carter

It is much easier and more convenient to focus on sins of which we are not known to be guilty.
Our Endangered Values by Jimmy Carter

Almost invariably, fundamentalist movements are led by authoritarian males who consider themselves to be superior to others and, within religious groups, have an overwhelming commitment to
Our Endangered Values by Jimmy Carter

Muhammad Yunus

Prize Motivation: "*for their efforts to create economic and social development from below*"
Prize Year: *2006*
Prize Category: *Peace*
Source: nobelprize.org

I am in favor of strengthening the freedom of the market. At the same time, I am very unhappy about the conceptual restrictions imposed on the players in the market. This originates from the assumption that entrepreneurs are one-dimensional human beings, who are dedicated to one mission in their business lives – to maximize profit. This interpretation of capitalism insulates the entrepreneurs from all political, emotional, social, spiritual, environmental dimensions of their lives. This was done perhaps as a reasonable simplification, but it stripped away the very essentials of human life. Human beings are a wonderful creation embodied with limitless human qualities and capabilities. Our theoretical constructs should make room for the blossoming of those qualities, not assume them away.
"Muhammad Yunus - Nobel Lecture". Nobelprize.org. 20 Nov 2012

The first thing I did was to try to persuade the bank located in the campus to lend money to the poor. But that did not work. The bank said that the poor were not creditworthy. After all my efforts, over several months, failed I offered to become a guarantor for the loans to the poor. I was stunned by the result. The poor paid back their loans, on time, every time! But still I kept confronting difficulties in expanding the program through the existing banks. That was when I decided to create a separate bank for the poor, and in 1983, I finally succeeded in doing that. I named it Grameen Bank or Village bank.
Today, Grameen Bank gives loans to nearly 7.0 million poor people, 97 per cent of whom are women, in 73,000 villages in Bangladesh. Grameen Bank gives collateral-free income generating, housing, student and micro-enterprise loans to the poor families and offers a host of attractive savings, pension funds and insurance products for its members. Since it introduced them in 1984, housing loans have been used to construct 640,000 houses. The legal ownership of these houses belongs to the women themselves. We focused on women because we found giving loans to women always brought more benefits to the family.
"Muhammad Yunus - Nobel Lecture". Nobelprize.org. 20 Nov 2012

I became involved in the poverty issue not as a policymaker or a researcher. I became involved because poverty was all around me, and I could not turn away from it. In 1974, I found it difficult to teach elegant theories of economics in the university classroom, in the backdrop of a terrible famine in Bangladesh. Suddenly, I felt the emptiness of those theories in the face of crushing hunger and poverty. I wanted to do something immediate to help people around me, even if it was just one human being, to get through another day with a little more ease. That brought me face to face with poor people's struggle to find the tiniest amounts of money to support their efforts to eke out a living

"Muhammad Yunus - Nobel Lecture". Nobelprize.org. 20 Nov 2012

Poverty is the absence of all human rights. The frustrations, hostility and anger generated by abject poverty cannot sustain peace in any society. For building stable peace we must find ways to provide opportunities for people to live decent lives.

"Muhammad Yunus - Nobel Lecture". Nobelprize.org. 20 Nov 2012

Peace should be understood in a human way – in a broad social, political and economic way. Peace is threatened by unjust economic, social and political order, absence of democracy, environmental degradation and absence of human rights.

"Muhammad Yunus - Nobel Lecture". Nobelprize.org. 20 Nov 2012

I believe terrorism cannot be won over by military action. Terrorism must be condemned in the strongest language. We must stand solidly against it, and find all the means to end it. We must address the root causes of terrorism to end it for all time to come. I believe that putting resources into improving the lives of the poor people is a better strategy than spending it on guns.

"Muhammad Yunus - Nobel Lecture". Nobelprize.org. 20 Nov 2012

Poverty is a threat to peace. The world's income distribution gives a very telling story. Ninety four percent of the world income goes to 40 percent of the population while sixty percent of people live on only 6 per cent of world income. Half of the world population lives on two dollars a day. Over one billion people live on less than a dollar a day. This is no formula for peace.

"Muhammad Yunus - Nobel Lecture". Nobelprize.org. 20 Nov 2012

The one message that we are trying to promote all the time, that poverty in the world is an artificial creation. It doesn't belong to human civilization, and we can change that, we can make people come out of poverty and have the real state of affairs. So the only thing we have to do is to redesign our institutions and policies, and there will be no people who will be suffering from poverty.

"Muhammad Yunus - Interview". Nobelprize.org. 15 Nov 2012

The more money we lent to poor women, the more I realized that credit given to a woman brings about change faster than when given to a man.
Banker to the Poor: Micro-Lending and the Battle Against World Poverty by Muhammad Yunus

When we want to help the poor, we usually offer them charity. Most often we use charity to avoid recognizing the problem and finding a solution for it. Charity becomes a way to shrug off our responsibility. But charity is no solution to poverty. Charity only perpetuates poverty by taking the initiative away from the poor. Charity allows us to go ahead with our own lives without worrying about the lives of the poor. Charity appeases our consciences.
Banker to the Poor: Micro-Lending and the Battle Against World Poverty by Muhammad Yunus

To my great surprise, the repayment of loans by people who borrow without collateral has proven to be much better than those whose borrowings are secured by assets. Indeed, more than 98 percent of our loans are repaid. The poor know that this credit is their only opportunity to break out of poverty. They do not have any cushion whatsoever to fall back on. If they fall afoul of this one loan, they will have lost their one and only chance to get out of the rut.
Banker to the Poor: Micro-Lending and the Battle Against World Poverty by Muhammad Yunus

When a destitute mother starts earning an income, her dreams of success invariably center around her children. A woman's second priority is the household. She wants to buy utensils, build a stronger roof, or find a bed for herself and her family. A man has an entirely different set of priorities. When a destitute father earns extra income, he focuses more attention on himself. Thus money entering a household through a woman brings more benefits to the family as a whole.
Banker to the Poor: Micro-Lending and the Battle Against World Poverty by Muhammad Yunus

In a social business an investor aims to help others without making any financial gain himself. The social business is a business because it must be self-sustaining—that is, it generates enough income to cover its own costs. Part of the economic surplus the social business creates is invested in expanding the business, and a part is kept in reserve to cover uncertainties. Thus, the social business might be described as a "non-loss, non-dividend company," dedicated entirely to achieving a social goal.
Building Social Business: The New Kind of Capitalism That Serves Humanity's Most Pressing Needs by Muhammad Yunus

Immerse yourself in the culture of the people you intend to serve.
Building Social Business: The New Kind of Capitalism That Serves Humanity's Most Pressing Needs by Muhammad Yunus

We must replace the one-dimensional person in economic theory with a multidimensional person—a person who has both selfish and selfless interests at the same time.

Building Social Business: The New Kind of Capitalism That Serves Humanity's Most Pressing Needs by Muhammad Yunus

Mainstream free-market theory suffers from a "conceptualization failure," a failure to capture the essence of what it is to be human.

Creating a World Without Poverty: Social Business and the Future of Capitalism by Muhammad Yunus

I believe in free markets as sources of inspiration and freedom for all, not as architects of decadence for a small elite.

Creating a World Without Poverty: Social Business and the Future of Capitalism by Muhammad Yunus

Barack H. Obama

Prize Motivation: "*for his extraordinary efforts to strengthen international diplomacy and cooperation between peoples*"
Prize Year: *2009*
Prize Category: *Peace*
Source: nobelprize.org

With hope and virtue, let us brave once more the icy currents, and endure what storms may come. Let it be said by our children's children that when we were tested we refused to let this journey end, that we did not turn back nor did we falter; and with eyes fixed on the horizon and God's grace upon us, we carried forth that great gift of freedom and delivered it safely to future generations.
Inaugural Address (2009)

Hope is the bedrock of this nation. The belief that our destiny will not be written for us, but by us, by all those men and women who are not content to settle for the world as it is, who have the courage to remake the world as it should be.
Iowa Caucus Victory Speech, Delivered at the Iowa Democratic caucus on 3 January 2008

For peace is not merely the absence of visible conflict. Only a just peace based on the inherent rights and dignity of every individual can truly be lasting.
"Barack H. Obama - Nobel Lecture: A Just and Lasting Peace". Nobelprize.org. 18 Nov 2012

But we do not have to think that human nature is perfect for us to still believe that the human condition can be perfected. We do not have to live in an idealized world to still reach for those ideals that will make it a better place. The non-violence practiced by men like Gandhi and King may not have been practical or possible in every circumstance, but the love that they preached – their fundamental faith in human progress – that must always be the North Star that guides us on our journey.
"Barack H. Obama - Nobel Lecture: A Just and Lasting Peace". Nobelprize.org. 18 Nov 2012

We can acknowledge that oppression will always be with us, and still strive for justice. We can admit the intractability of depravation, and still strive for dignity. Clear-eyed, we can understand that there will be war, and still strive for peace. We can do that – for that is the story of human progress; that's the hope of all the world; and at this moment of challenge, that must be our work here on Earth.
"Barack H. Obama - Nobel Lecture: A Just and Lasting Peace". Nobelprize.org. 18 Nov 2012

Let us reach for the world that ought to be – that spark of the divine that still stirs within each of our souls.
"Barack H. Obama - Nobel Lecture: A Just and Lasting Peace". Nobelprize.org. 18 Nov 2012

For if we lose that faith – if we dismiss it as silly or naïve; if we divorce it from the decisions that we make on issues of war and peace – then we lose what's best about humanity. We lose our sense of possibility. We lose our moral compass.
"Barack H. Obama - Nobel Lecture: A Just and Lasting Peace". Nobelprize.org. 18 Nov 2012

My identity might begin with the fact of my race, but it didn't, couldn't, end there.
Dreams from My Father: A Story of Race and Inheritance by Barack Obama

No one is exempt from the call to find common ground.
The Audacity of Hope: Thoughts on Reclaiming the American Dream by Barack Obama

By these standards at least, it sometimes appears that Americans today value nothing so much as being rich, thin, young, famous, safe, and entertained. We say we value the legacy we leave the next generation and then saddle that generation with mountains of debt. We say we believe in equal opportunity but then stand idle while millions of American children languish in poverty. We insist that we value family, but then structure our economy and organize our lives so as to ensure that our families get less and less of our time.
The Audacity of Hope: Thoughts on Reclaiming the American Dream by Barack Obama

Physiology or Medicine Nobel Laureates

Albert von Szent-Györgyi Nagyrápolt

Prize Motivation: "*for his discoveries in connection with the biological combustion processes, with special reference to vitamin C and the catalysis of fumaric acid*"
Prize Year: *1937*
Prize Category: *Physiology or Medicine*
Source: *nobelprize.org*

A discovery must be, by definition, at variance with existing knowledge. During my lifetime, I made two. Both were rejected offhand by the popes of the field. Had I predicted these discoveries in my applications, and had those authorities been my judges, it is evident what their decisions would have been.
In 'Dionysians and Apollonians', Science (2 Jun 1972), 176, 966. Reprinted in Mary Ritchie Key, The Relationship of Verbal and Nonverbal Communication (1980), 318.

All living organisms are but leaves on the same tree of life. The various functions of plants and animals and their specialized organs are manifestations of the same living matter. This adapts itself to different jobs and circumstances, but operates on the same basic principles. Muscle contraction is only one of these adaptations. In principle it would not matter whether we studied nerve, kidney or muscle to understand the basic principles of life. In practice, however, it matters a great deal.
'Muscle Research', Scientific American, 1949, 180 (6), 22.

Discovery consists of seeing what everybody has seen and thinking what nobody has thought.
Bioenergetics Part 2, 57. Quoted in I.J. Good, The Scientist Speculates (1963), 15.

I always tried to live up to Leo Szilard's commandment, 'don't lie if you don't have to.' I had to. I filled up pages with words and plans I knew I would not follow. When I go home from my laboratory in the late afternoon, I often do not know what I am going to do the next day. I expect to think that up during the night. How could I tell them what I would do a year hence?
In 'Dionysians and Apollonians', Science (2 Jun 1972), 176, 966. Reprinted in Mary Ritchie Key, The Relationship of Verbal and Nonverbal Communication (1980), 318.

If any student comes to me and says he wants to be useful to mankind and go into research to alleviate human suffering, I advise him to go into charity instead. Research wants real egotists who seek their own pleasure and satisfaction, but find it in solving the puzzles of nature.
In Science Today (May 1980), 35. In Vladimir Burdyuzha, The Future of Life and the Future of Our Civilization (2006), 374.

If I go out into nature, into the unknown, to the fringes of knowledge, everything seems mixed up and contradictory, illogical, and incoherent. This is what research does; it smooths out contradictions and makes things simple, logical, and coherent.

In 'Dionysians and Apollonians', Science (2 Jun 1972), 176, 966. Reprinted in Mary Ritchie Key, The Relationship of Verbal and Nonverbal Communication (1980), 318.

If Louis Pasteur were to come out of his grave because he heard that the cure for cancer still had not been found, NIH would tell him, "Of course we'll give you assistance. Now write up exactly what you will be doing during the three years of your grant." Pasteur would say, "Thank you very much," and would go back to his grave. Why? Because research means going into the unknown. If you know what you are going to do in science, then you are stupid! This is like telling Michelangelo or Renoir that he must tell you in advance how many reds and how many blues he will buy, and exactly how he will put those colors together.

Interview for Saturday Evening Post (Jan/Feb 1981), 30.

Life is water, dancing to the tune of solids.

From Perspect. Biol. Med. (1971), 12, 239. As cited by John G Watterson, 'The Wave-Cluster Model of Water-Protein Interactions', in David G Green, Complex Systems: From Biology to Computation (1993), 36. Also quoted as "Life is water, dancing to the tune of macro molecules," by Gerald H. Pollack and Ivan L. Cameron, in Water and the Cell (2006), viii.

One death is a tragedy, 100,000 deaths are statistics.

The Crazy Ape (1970), 29.

Through the ages, man's main concern was life after death. Today, for the first time, we find we must ask questions about whether there will be life before death.

The Crazy Ape (1970), 18.

To regulate something always requires two opposing factors. You cannot regulate by a single factor. To give an example, the traffic in the streets could not be controlled by a green light or a red light alone. It needs a green light and a red light as well. The ratio between retine and promine determines whether there is any motion, any growth, or not. Two different inclinations have to be there in readiness to make the cells proliferate.

In Ralph W. Moss, Free Radical (1988), 186.

When I received the Nobel Prize, the only big lump sum of money I have ever seen, I had to do something with it. The easiest way to drop this hot potato was to invest it, to buy shares. I knew that World War II was coming and I was afraid that if I had shares which rise in case of war, I would wish for war. So I asked my agent to buy shares which go down in the event of war. This he did. I lost my money and saved my soul.

In The Crazy Ape (1970), 21.

Francis Harry Compton Crick

Prize Motivation: "*for their discoveries concerning the molecular structure of nucleic acids and its significance for information transfer in living material*"
Prize Year: *1962*
Prize Category: *Physiology or Medicine*
Source: nobelprize.org

A busy life is a wasted life.
What Mad Pursuit: A Personal View of Scientific Discovery (1988), 145.

Again the message to experimentalists is: Be sensible but don't be impressed too much by negative arguments. If at all possible, try it and see what turns up. Theorists almost always dislike this sort of approach.
What mad pursuit: a personal view of scientific discovery (1988), 113.

Almost all aspects of life are engineered at the molecular level, and without understanding molecules we can only have a very sketchy understanding of life itself.
What Mad Pursuit: A Personal View of Scientific Discovery (1988), 61.

Chance is the only source of true novelty.
Life Itself: Its Origin and Nature (1982), 58.

Exact knowledge is the enemy of vitalism.
In Of Molecules and Men (1966, 2004), prefatory statement.

Haemoglobin is a very large molecule by ordinary standards, containing about ten thousand atoms, but the chances are that your haemoglobin and mine are identical, and significantly different from that of a pig or horse. You may be impressed by how much human beings differ from one another, but if you were to look into the fine details of the molecules of which they are constructed, you would be astonished by their similarity.
In Of Molecules and Men (1966, 2004), 6.

It is notoriously difficult to define the word living.
Opening sentence in Of Molecules and Men (1966, 2004), 3.

There is no form of prose more difficult to understand and more tedious to read than the average scientific paper.
The Astonishing Hypothesis: The Scientific Search for the Soul (1995), xiii.

To produce a really good biological theory one must try to see through the clutter produced by evolution to the basic mechanisms lying beneath them, realizing that they are likely to be overlaid by other, secondary mechanisms. What seems to physicists to be a hopelessly complicated process may have been what nature found simplest, because nature could only build on what was already there.
What Mad Pursuit (1990), 139.

[Science has shown you that] 'you,' your joys and your sorrows, your memories and your ambitions, your sense of identity and free will, are in fact no more than the behaviour of a vast assembly of nerve cells and their associated molecules. as Lewis Carroll's Alice might have phrased it: 'You're nothing but a pack of neurons.'
The Astonishing Hypothesis: The Scientific Search for Soul (1994), 3.

Gerald M. Edelman

Prize Motivation: "*for their discoveries concerning the chemical structure of antibodies*"
Prize Year: *1972*
Prize Category: *Physiology or Medicine*
Source: *nobelprize.org*

...most of the scientists who ever existed are alive today.
"Gerald M. Edelman - Banquet Speech". Nobelprize.org. 15 Nov 2012Commenting on the compression of time in our age.

Science is imagination in the service of the verifiable truth and that service is indeed communal. It cannot be rigidly planned. Rather, it requires freedom and courage and the plural contributions of many different kinds of people who must maintain their individuality while giving to the group.
Gerald M. Edelman - Banquet Speech". Nobelprize.org. 15 Nov 2012

It is nearly impossible for us as humans to revert to or even contemplate a state of consciousness that is completely free of the self. In ether words, we are agents, aware of being aware, and aware that we are making decisions that are based on our histories and plans.
A Universe Of Consciousness How Matter Becomes Imagination by Gerald Edelman, Giulio Tononi

Doing and Understanding. A biological observation that is also connected to the evolutionary assumption is that during learning and in many matters of human comprehension, doing generally precedes understanding.
A Universe Of Consciousness How Matter Becomes Imagination by Gerald Edelman, Giulio Tononi

If our scientific description of the world is concerned with nature, our creativity reflects the ability of our brain to give rise to a second nature.
Second Nature: Brain Science and Human Knowledge by Gerald M. Edelman

The capacity to develop concepts of the past and future and to acquire a social self depends very strongly on the acquisition of language.
Second Nature: Brain Science and Human Knowledge by Gerald M. Edelman

A knowledge of brain science will provide one of the major foundations of the new age to come. That knowledge will spawn cures for disease, new machines based on brain function, further insights into our nature and how we know.
Second Nature: Brain Science and Human Knowledge Gerald M. Edelman Second Nature: Brain Science and Human Knowledge (2006)

Higher-order consciousness confers the ability to imagine the future, explicitly recall the past, and to be conscious of being conscious.
Wider Than the Sky: A Revolutionary View of Consciousness (Penguin Press Science) by Gerald M. Edelman

Thus, each event of memory is dynamic and context-sensitive—it yields a repetition of a mental or physical act that is similar but not identical to previous acts. It is recategorical: it does not replicate an original experience exactly.
Wider Than the Sky: A Revolutionary View of Consciousness (Penguin Press Science) by Gerald M. Edelman

Looked at from the inside, consciousness seems continually to change, yet at each moment it is all of piece—what I have called "the remembered present"—reflecting the fact that all my past experience is engaged in forming my integrated awareness of this single moment.
Wider than the Sky: The Phenomenal Gift of Consciousness by Gerald Edelman

Konrad Lorenz

Prize Motivation: "*for their discoveries concerning organization and elicitation of individual and social behaviour patterns*"
Prize Year: *1973*
Prize Category: *Physiology or Medicine*
Source: nobelprize.org

We are the highest achievement reached so far by the great constructors of evolution. We are their "latest" but certainly not their last word. The scientist must not regard anything as absolute, not even the laws of pure reason. He must remain aware of the great fact, discovered by Heraclitus, that nothing whatever really remains the same even for one moment, but that everything is perpetually changing. To regard man, the most ephemeral and rapidly evolving of all species, as the final and unsurpassable achievement of creation, especially at his present-day particularly dangerous and disagreeable stage of development, is certainly the most arrogant and dangerous of all untenable doctrines. If I thought of man as the final image of God, I should not know what to think of God. But when I consider that our ancestors, at a time fairly recent in relation to the earth's history, were perfectly ordinary apes, closely related to chimpanzees, I see a glimmer of hope. It does not require very great optimism to assume that from us human beings something better and higher may evolve. Far from seeing in man the irrevocable and unsurpassable image of God, I assert – more modestly and, I believe, in greater awe of the Creation and its infinite possibilities – that the long-sought missing link between animals and the really humane being is ourselves!
In On Aggression (2002), Ch. XII : On the Virtue of Scientific Humility.

I believe—and human psychologists, particularly psychoanalysts should test this—that present-day civilized man suffers from insufficient discharge of his aggressive drive. It is more than probable that the evil effects of the human aggressive drives, explained by Sigmund Freud as the results of a special death wish, simply derive from the fact that in prehistoric times intra-specific selection bred into man a measure of aggression drive for which in the social order today he finds no adequate outlet.
On Aggression, trans. M. Latzke (1966), 209.

Scientific truth is universal, because it is only discovered by the human brain and not made by it, as art is.
In On Aggression (2002), 279.

The truth about nature is always far more beautiful even than what our great poets sing of.
King Solomon's Ring by Konrad Lorenz

How thankful I should be to fate, if I could find but one path which, generations after me, might be trodden by fellowmembers of my species. And how infinitely grateful I should be, if, in my life's work, I could find one small "up-current" which might lift some other scientist to a point from which he could see a little further than I do.
King Solomon's Ring by Konrad Lorenz

But have not we human beings also such blind, instinctive reactions? Do not whole peoples all too often react with a blind rage to a mere dummy presented to them by the artifice of the demagogue? Is not this dummy in many cases just as far from being a real enemy as were my black bathing drawers to the jackdaws? And would there still be wars, if all this were not so?
King Solomon's Ring by Konrad Lorenz

I do not know whether I have made it quite clear how very remarkable all this is: an animal which does not know its enemy by innate instinct, is informed by older and more experienced fellow-members of its species who or what is to be feared as hostile. This is true tradition, the handing-down of personally acquired knowledge from one generation to another.
King Solomon's Ring by Konrad Lorenz

When, in the course of its evolution, a species of animals develops a weapon which may destroy a fellow-member at one blow, then, in order to survive, it must develop, along with the weapon, a social inhibition to prevent a usage which could endanger the existence of the species.
King Solomon's Ring by Konrad Lorenz

The superficial similarity between these animal utterances and human languages diminishes further as it becomes gradually clear to the observer that the animal, in all these sounds and movements expressing its emotions, has in no way the conscious intention of influencing a fellow-member of its species.
King Solomon's Ring by Konrad Lorenz

Believe me, I am not mistakenly assigning human properties to animals: on the contrary, I am showing you what an enormous animal inheritance remains in man, to this day.
King Solomon's Ring by Konrad Lorenz

The bond with a true dog is as lasting as the ties of this earth will ever be.
Man Meets Dog Konrad Lorenz Man Meets Dog (1949)

All social animals are 'status seekers', hence there is always particularly high tension between individuals who hold immediately adjoining positions in the ranking order; conversely, this tension diminishes the farther apart the two animals are in rank.
On Aggression (Routledge Classics) by Konrad Lorenz

There is no love without aggression, but there is no hate without love!
On Aggression (Routledge Classics) by Konrad Lorenz

Knowledge springing from conceptual thought robbed man of the security provided by his well-adapted instincts long, long before it was sufficient to provide him with an equally safe adaptation.
On Aggression (Routledge Classics) by Konrad Lorenz

We do not know of a single animal which is capable of personal friendship and which lacks aggression.
On Aggression (Routledge Classics) by Konrad Lorenz

Among animals symbols are not transmitted by tradition from generation to generation, and it is here, if one wishes, that one may draw the border line between 'the animal' and man.
On Aggression (Routledge Classics) by Konrad Lorenz

Gertrude B. Elion

Prize Motivation: "*for their discoveries of important principles for drug treatment*"
Prize Year: *1988*
Prize Category: *Physiology or Medicine*
Source: nobelprize.org

It is important to go into work you would like to do. Then it doesn't seem like work. You sometimes feel it's almost too good to be true that someone will pay you for enjoying yourself. I've been very fortunate that my work led to useful drugs for a variety of serious illnesses. The thrill of seeing people get well who might otherwise have died of diseases like leukemia, kidney failure, and herpes virus encephalitis cannot be described in words.
Dr. Jonathan Elion, nephew

"The idea was to do research, find new avenues to conquer, new mountains to climb."
"Gertrude B. Elion: Interview (page: 5/7)". Academy of Achievement.

Don't be afraid of hard work. Nothing worthwhile comes easily. Don't let others discourage you or tell you that you can't do it. In my day I was told women didn't go into chemistry. I saw no reason why we couldn't.
from her lecture notes

I had fallen in love with a young man..., and we were planning to get married. And then he died of subacute bacterial endocarditis... Two years later with the advent of penicillin, he would have been saved. It reinforced in my mind the importance of scientific discovery...
Quoted in Susan Ambrose et al., Journeys of Women in Science and Engineering: No Universal Constants (1997)

I had no specific bent toward science until my grandfather died of stomach cancer. I decided that nobody should suffer that much.
Quoted in Azhar Saleem Virk, Inspiration from Lives of Famous People (2003).

I think it's a very valuable thing for a doctor to learn how to do research, to learn how to approach research, something there isn't time to teach them in medical school. They don't really learn how to approach a problem, and yet diagnosis is a problem; and I think that year spent in research is extremely valuable to them.On mentoring a medical student.
Quoted in interview by Mary Ellen Avery (1997)

Maybe I was young and 'cute' (after all, I was only twenty then), but I've learned over the years that when you put white lab coats on chemists, they all look alike!

(6 Jul 1989) recalling being denied a laboratory job in her youth, since - allegedly - her physical attractiveness would be distracting to male coworkers. quoted in Feminine Ingenuity by Anne L. MacDonald (1992)

People ask me often [whether] the Nobel Prize [was] the thing you were aiming for all your life, and I say that would be crazy. Nobody would aim for a Nobel Prize because, if you didn't get it, your whole life would be wasted. What we were aiming at was getting people well, and the satisfaction of that is much greater than any prize you can get.

Quoted in interview by Mary Ellen Avery (1997).

That was the turning point. It was as though the signal was there, 'This is the disease you're going to have to work against.' I never really stopped to think about anything else. It was that sudden.

Autobiography, Nobel Foundation

The Nobel Prize is fine, but the drugs I've developed are rewards in themselves.

Quoted in the New York Times (18 Oct 1988).

Eric R. Kandel

Prize Motivation: "*for their discoveries concerning signal transduction in the nervous system*"
Prize Year: *2000*
Prize Category: *Physiology or Medicine*
Source: nobelprize.org

The key principle that guides our work is that the mind is a set of operations carried out by the brain, an astonishingly complex computational device that constructs our perception of the external world, fixes our attention, and controls our actions.
"Eric R. Kandel - Banquet Speech". Nobelprize.org. 23 Nov 2012

The biological study of mind is more than a scientific inquiry of great promise; it is also an important humanistic endeavor. The biology of mind bridges the sciences - concerned with the natural world - and the humanities - concerned with the meaning of human experience. Insights that come from this new synthesis will not only improve our understanding of psychiatric and neurological disorders, but will also lead to a deeper understanding of ourselves.
"Eric R. Kandel - Banquet Speech". Nobelprize.org. 23 Nov 2012

How could a highly educated and cultured society, a society that at one historical moment nourished the music of Haydn, Mozart, and Beethoven, in the next historical moment sink into barbarism? Clearly the answer to this question is complex, and many scholars of this period have attempted partial answers. One conclusion, troubling to an academic like myself, is that a society's culture is not a reliable indicator of its respect for human life.
"Eric R. Kandel - Autobiography". Nobelprize.org. 23 Nov 2012

Without the binding force of memory, experience would be splintered into as many fragments as there are moments in life. Without the mental time travel provided by memory, we would have no awareness of our personal history, no way of remembering the joys that serve as the luminous milestones of our life. We are who we are because of what we learn and what we remember.
In Search of Memory: The Emergence of a New Science of Mind by Eric R. Kandel

Aristotle's and Locke's suggestion that learning involves the association of ideas was replaced by the empirical fact that learning occurs through the association of two stimuli or a stimulus and a response.
In Search of Memory: The Emergence of a New Science of Mind by Eric R. Kandel

Cultural evolution, a nonbiological mode of adaptation, acts in parallel with biological evolution as the means of transmitting knowledge of the past and adaptive behavior across generations. All human accomplishments, from antiquity to modern times, are products of a shared memory accumulated over centuries, whether through written records or through a carefully protected oral tradition.

In Search of Memory: The Emergence of a New Science of Mind by Eric R. Kandel

One of the fundamental features of memory is that it is formed in stages. Short-term memory lasts minutes, while long-term memory lasts many days or even longer. Behavioral experiments suggest that short-term memory grades naturally into long-term memory and, moreover, that it does so through repetition. Practice does make perfect.

In Search of Memory: The Emergence of a New Science of Mind by Eric R. Kandel

The new science of mind attempts to penetrate the mystery of consciousness, including the ultimate mystery: how each person's brain creates the consciousness of a unique self and the sense of free

In Search of Memory: The Emergence of a New Science of Mind by Eric R. Kandel

No aspect of mental activity is simply noise in the machinery of the brain. Mental events do not occur by chance, but adhere to scientific laws.

The Age of Insight: The Quest to Understand the Unconscious in Art, Mind, and Brain, from Vienna 1900 to the Present by Eric Kandel

Mental processes operate primarily unconsciously; conscious thought and emotion are the exception rather than the rule.

The Age of Insight: The Quest to Understand the Unconscious in Art, Mind, and Brain, from Vienna 1900 to the Present by Eric Kandel

Chemistry Nobel Laureates

Svante August Arrhenius

Prize Motivation: "*in recognition of the extraordinary services he has rendered to the advancement of chemistry by his electrolytic theory of dissociation*"
Prize Year: *1903*
Prize Category: *Chemistry*
Source: nobelprize.org

Since, now, warm ages have alternated with glacial periods, even after man appeared on the earth, we have to ask ourselves: Is it probable that we shall in the coming geological ages be visited by a new ice period that will drive us from our temperate countries into the hotter climates of Africa? There does not appear to be much ground for such an apprehension. The enormous combustion of coal by our industrial establishments suffices to increase the percentage of carbon dioxide in the air to a perceptible degree.
Världarnas utveckling (1906) (German: Das Werden der Welten [1907], English: Worlds in the Making [1908]

We often hear lamentations that the coal stored up in the earth is wasted by the present generation without any thought of the future, and we are terrified by the awful destruction of life and property which has followed the volcanic eruptions of our days. We may find a kind of consolation in the consideration that here, as in every other case, there is good mixed with the evil. By the influence of the increasing percentage of carbonic acid in the atmosphere, we may hope to enjoy ages with more equable and better climates, especially as regards the colder regions of the Earth, ages when the Earth will bring forth much more abundant crops than at present, for the benefit of rapidly propagating mankind.
Världarnas utveckling (1906) (German: Das Werden der Welten [1907], English: Worlds in the Making [1908]

Concern about our raw materials casts its dark shadow over mankind. Those states which lack [them] throw lustful glances at neighbours, which happen to have more than they use. Still more tempting is the desire for gain from lands on the other side of the seas, inhabited by uncivilized natives, with interest unawakened in guardianship.
Arrhenius, S. (1925) Chemistry in Modern Life, Library of Modern Sciences, D. Van Nostrand Company, New Jersey.Arrhenius saw the danger of resource wars, fearing a return to 'dark times' after the end of World War One.

Engineers must design more efficient internal combustion engines capable of running on alternative fuels such as alcohol, and new research into battery power should be undertaken... Wind motors and solar engines hold great promise and would reduce the level of CO2 emissions. Forests must be planted... To conserve coal, half a tonne of which is burned in transporting the other half tonne to market... so the building of power plants should be in close proximity to the mines... All lighting with petroleum products should be replaced with more efficient electric lamps.

Arrhenius, S. (1925) Chemistry in Modern Life, Library of Modern Sciences, D. Van Nostrand Company, New Jersey.

Like insane wastrels, we spend that which we received in legacy from our fathers. Our descendants surely will sensor us for having squandered their just birthright... Statesman can plead no excuse for letting development go on to the point where mankind will run the danger of the end of natural resources in a few hundred years.

Arrhenius, S. (1925) Chemistry in Modern Life, Library of Modern Sciences, D. Van Nostrand Company, New Jersey.

A hundred years ago, Swedish scientist Svante Arrhenius asked the important question "Is the mean temperature of the ground in any way influenced by the presence of the heat-absorbing gases in the atmosphere?" He went on to become the first person to investigate the effect that doubling atmospheric carbon dioxide would have on global climate. His research contributed to our understanding of the greenhouse effect.

The Earth Observatory, part of the EOS Project Science Office located at NASA Goddard Space Flight Center

At first sight nothing seems more obvious than that everything has a beginning and an end, and that everything can be subdivided into smaller parts. Nevertheless, for entirely speculative reasons the philosophers of Antiquity, especially the Stoics, concluded this concept to be quite unnecessary. The prodigious development of physics has now reached the same conclusion as those philosophers, Empedocles and Democritus in particular, who lived around 500 B.C. and for whom even ancient man had a lively admiration.

'Development of the Theory of Electrolytic Dissociation', Nobel Lecture, 11 December 1903. In Nobel Lectures: Chemistry 1901-1921 (1966), 45.

Chemistry works with an enormous number of substances, but cares only for some few of their properties; it is an extensive science. Physics on the other hand works with rather few substances, such as mercury, water, alcohol, glass, air, but analyses the experimental results very thoroughly; it is an intensive science. Physical chemistry is the child of these two sciences; it has inherited the extensive character from chemistry. Upon this depends its all-embracing feature, which has attracted so great admiration. But on the other hand it has its profound quantitative character from the science of physics.
In Theories of Solutions (1912), xix.

Humanity stands ... before a great problem of finding new raw materials and new sources of energy that shall never become exhausted. In the meantime we must not waste what we have, but must leave as much as possible for coming generations.
Chemistry in Modern Life (1925), trans. Clifford Shattuck-Leonard, vii.

In a great number of the cosmogonic myths the world is said to have developed from a great water, which was the prime matter. In many cases, as for instance in an Indian myth, this prime matter is indicated as a solution, out of which the solid earth crystallized out.
In Theories of Solutions (1912), 1.

Ernest Rutherford

Prize Motivation: "*for his investigations into the disintegration of the elements, and the chemistry of radioactive substances*"
Prize Year: *1908*
Prize Category: *Chemistry*
Source: nobelprize.org

I am a great believer in the simplicity of things and as you probably know I am inclined to hang on to broad & simple ideas like grim death until evidence is too strong for my tenacity.
Letter to Irving Langmuir (10 Jun 1919). Quoted in Nathan Reingold and Ida H. Reingold, Science in America: A Documentary History 1900-1939 (1981), 354.

I think a strong claim can be made that the process of scientific discovery may be regarded as a form of art. This is best seen in the theoretical aspects of Physical Science. The mathematical theorist builds up on certain assumptions and according to well understood logical rules, step by step, a stately edifice, while his imaginative power brings out clearly the hidden relations between its parts. A well constructed theory is in some respects undoubtedly an artistic production. A fine example is the famous Kinetic Theory of Maxwell. ... The theory of relativity by Einstein, quite apart from any question of its validity, cannot but be regarded as a magnificent work of art.Responding to the toast, 'Science!' at the Royal Academy of the Arts in 1932.)
Quoted in Lawrence Badash, 'Ernest Rutherford and Theoretical Physics,' in Robert Kargon and Peter Achinstein (eds.) Kelvin's Baltimore Lectures and Modern Theoretical Physics: Historical and Philosophical Perspectives (1987), 352.

It is not the nature of things for any one man to make a sudden, violent discovery; science goes step by step and every man depends on the work of his predecessors. When you hear of a sudden unexpected discovery - a bolt from the blue - you can always be sure that it has grown up by the influence of one man or another, and it is the mutual influence which makes the enormous possibility of scientific advance. Scientists are not dependent on the ideas of a single man, but on the combined wisdom of thousands of men, all thinking of the same problem and each doing his little bit to add to the great structure of knowledge which is gradually being erected.
Quoted in Robert B. Heywood, 'The Works of the Mind', The Scientist (1947), 178.

We haven't the money, so we've got to think.
Quoted by R. V. Jones, Bulletin of the Institute of Physics (1962), 13, No.4, 102.

If your result needs a statistician then you should design a better experiment.
Unknown

The only possible interpretation of any research whatever in the 'social sciences' is: some do, some don't.
Unknown

We've got no money, so we've got to think.
As quoted in Quips, Quotes, and Quanta : An Anecdotal History of Physics (2007) by Anton Z. Capri, page 65.

When we have found how the nucleus of atoms is built up we shall have found the greatest secret of all — except life. We shall have found the basis of everything — of the earth we walk on, of the air we breathe, of the sunshine, of our physical body itself, of everything in the world, however great or however small — except life.
As quoted in The Wit and Wisdom of the 20th Century : A Dictionary of Quotations (1987) by Frank S. Pepper, p. 226

An alleged scientific discovery has no merit unless it can be explained to a barmaid.
As quoted in Einstein: The Man and His Achievement (1973) by G. J. Whitrow, p. 42

All science is either physics or stamp collecting.
As quoted in Rutherford at Manchester (1962) by J. B. Birks Unsourced variants: That which is not measurable is not science. That which is not physics is stamp collecting. Physics is the only real science. The rest are just stamp collecting. That which is not measurable is not science. — (which is also attributed to Lord Kelvin)

Frederick Soddy

Prize Motivation: "*for his contributions to our knowledge of the chemistry of radioactive substances, and his investigations into the origin and nature of isotopes*"
Prize Year: *1921*
Prize Category: *Chemistry*
Source: nobelprize.org

The catastrophe [World War I] which has recently engulfed the world has, however, not been without its own intellectual renaissance. The effects are not yet apparent, but, at least, perhaps not all of us are now totally blind to the dangers ahead, or to the need of that impersonal but remorseless re-examination of the foundations of society, which Science has already applied to the mechanism of the physical universe. Possibly it may fail. Perhaps it may be too late. Even so, yet I cherish the fancy that, whatever may happen in the crowded and fevered countries that are still ranged in fratricidal animosity, here at least, here in the Northlands, truth will endure.
"Frederick Soddy - Banquet Speech". Nobelprize.org. 15 Nov 2012

As scientific men we have all, no doubt, felt that our work has been put often to base uses, which must lead to disaster. But what sin is to the moralist and crime to the jurist so to the scientific man is ignorance. On our plane knowledge and ignorance are the immemorial adversaries.
Scientific men can hardly escape the charge of ignorance with regard to the precise effect of the impact of modern science upon the mode of living of the people and upon their civilisation. For them, such a charge is worse than that of crime.

"Frederick Soddy - Banquet Speech". Nobelprize.org. 15 Nov 2012

For a modern ruler the laws of conservation and transformation of energy, when the vivifing stream takes its source, the ways it wends its course in nature, and how, under wisdom and knowledge, it may be intertwined with human destiny, instead of careering headlong to the ocean, are a study at least as pregnant with consequences to life as any lesson taught by the long unscientific history of man.
Science and Life (1920), 5.

The dropping of the Atomic Bomb is a very deep problem... Instead of commemorating Hiroshima we should celebrate... man's triumph over the problem [of transmutation], and not its first misuse by politicians and military authorities.
Address to New Europe Group meeting on the third anniversary of the Hiroshima bomb. Quoted in New Europe Group, In Commemoration of Professor Frederick Soddy (1956), 6-7.

The energy available for each individual man is his income, and the philosophy which can teach him to be content with penury should be capable of teaching him also the uses of wealth.
Science and Life: Aberdeen Addresses (1920), 6.

The fact remains that, if the supply of energy failed, modern civilization would come to an end as abruptly as does the music of an organ deprived of wind. [But] ... the still unrecognized 'energy problem' ... awaits the future.
Matter and Energy (1912), 251.

The history of man is dominated by, and reflects, the amount of available energy
Science and Life (1920), 7.

The laws expressing the relations between energy and matter are, however, not solely of importance in pure science. They necessarily come first in order ... in the whole record of human experience, and they control, in the last resort, the rise or fall of political systems, the freedom or bondage of nations, the movements of commerce and industry, the origin of wealth and poverty, and the general physical welfare of the race.
In Matter and Energy (1912), 10-11.

The real value of science is in the getting, and those who have tasted the pleasure of discovery alone know what science is. A problem solved is dead. A world without problems to be solved would be devoid of science.
In Matter and Energy (1912), 18.

There has been no discovery like it in the history of man. It puts into man's hands the key to using the fundamental energy of the universe.
Address to New Europe Group meeting on the third anniversary of the Hiroshima bomb. Quoted in New Europe Group, In Commemoration of Professor Frederick Soddy (1956), 7.

[The blame for the future 'plight of civilization] must rest on scientific men, equally with others, for being incapable of accepting the responsibility for the profound social upheavals which their own work primarily has brought about in human relationships.
Quoted in Thaddeus Trenn, 'The Central Role of Energy in Soddy's Holistic and Critical Approach to Nuclear Science, Economics, and Social Responsibility', British Journal for the History of Science (1979), 42, 261.

Linus Carl Pauling

Prize Motivation: "*for his research into the nature of the chemical bond and its application to the elucidation of the structure of complex substances*"
Prize Year: *1954*
Prize Category: *Chemistry*
Source: nobelprize.org

I have something that I call my Golden Rule. It goes something like this: "Do unto others twenty-five percent better than you expect them to do unto you." … The twenty-five percent is for error.
Pauling's reply to an audience question about his ethical system, following his lecture circa 1961 at Monterey Peninsula College, in Monterey, California.

When an old and distinguished person speaks to you, listen to him carefully and with respect — but do not believe him. Never put your trust into anything but your own intellect. Your elder, no matter whether he has gray hair or has lost his hair, no matter whether he is a Nobel laureate — may be wrong. The world progresses, year by year, century by century, as the members of the younger generation find out what was wrong among the things that their elders said. So you must always be skeptical — always think for yourself.
Linus Pauling: Scientist and Peacemaker (2001) by Clifford Mead and Thomas Hager

Only when I began studying chemical engineering at Oregon Agricultural College did I realize that I myself might discover something new about the nature of the world.
Linus Pauling In His Own Words (1995) by Barbara Marinacci

If you want to have good ideas you must have many ideas. Most of them will be wrong, and what you have to learn is which ones to throw away.
As quoted by Francis Crick in his presentation "The Impact of Linus Pauling on Molecular Biology" (1995)

I've been asked from time to time, "How does it happen that you have made so many discoveries? Are you smarter than other scientists?" And my answer has been that I am sure that I am not smarter than other scientists. I don't have any precise evaluation of my IQ, but to the extent that psychologists have said that my IQ is about 160, I recognize that there are one hundred thousand or more people in the United States that have IQs higher than that. So I have said that I think I think harder, think more than other people do, than other scientists. That is, for years, almost all of my thinking was about science and scientific problems that I was interested in.
Interview at Big Sur, California (11 November 1990)

Science cannot be stopped. Man will gather knowledge no matter what the consequences – and we cannot predict what they will be. Science will go on — whether we are pessimistic, or are optimistic, as I am. I know that great, interesting, and valuable discoveries can be made and will be made... But I know also that still more interesting discoveries will be made that I have not the imagination to describe — and I am awaiting them, full of curiosity and enthusiasm.
Lecture at Yale University, "Chemical Achievement and Hope for the Future." (October 1947) Published in Science in Progress. Sixth Series. Ed. George A. Baitsell. 100-21, (1949)

[Instead of collecting stamps, he collected dictionaries and encyclopaedias:] Because you can learn more from them.
'Dr Linus Pauling, Atomic Architect', Science Illustrated (1948), 3, 40.

I have been especially fortunate for about 50 years in having two memory banks available—whenever I can't remember something I ask my wife, and thus I am able to draw on this auxiliary memory bank. Moreover, there is a second way In which I get ideas ... I listen carefully to what my wife says, and in this way I often get a good idea. I recommend to ... young people ... that you make a permanent acquisition of an auxiliary memory bank that you can become familiar with and draw upon throughout your lives.
T. Goertzel and B. Goertzel, Linus Pauling (1995), 240.

I try to identify myself with the atoms ... I ask what I would do If I were a carbon atom or a sodium atom.
Comment made to George Gray (Rockefeller's resident science writer and publicist). Quoted In Thomas Hager, Force of Nature: The Life of Linus Pauling (1995), 377.

Life ... is a relationship between molecules.
Quoted In T. Hager, Force of Nature: The Life of Linus Pauling (1997), 542.

Men will gather knowledge no matter what the consequences. Science will go on whether we are pessimistic or optimistic, as I am. More interesting discoveries than we can imagine will be made, and I am awaiting them, full of curiosity and enthusiasm.
'Dr Linus Pauling, Atomic Architect', Science Illustrated (1948), 3, 40.

You have to have a lot of ideas. First, if you want to make discoveries, it's a good thing to have good ideas. And second, you have to have a sort of sixth sense—the result of judgment and experience—which ideas are worth following up. I seem to have the first thing, a lot of ideas, and I also seem to have good judgment as to which are the bad ideas that I should just ignore, and the good ones, that I'd better follow up.
As quoted by Nancy Rouchette, The Journal of NIH Research (Jul 1990), 2, 63. Reprinted in Linus Pauling, Barclay Kamb, Linus Pauling: Selected Scientific Papers, Vol. 2, Biomolecular Sciences (2001), 1101.

Max Ferdinand Perutz

Prize Motivation: "*for their studies of the structures of globular proteins*"
Prize Year: *1962*
Prize Category: *Chemistry*
Source: *nobelprize.org*

True science thrives best in glass houses where everyone can look in. When the windows are blacked out, as in war, the weeds take over; when secrecy muffles criticism, charlatans and cranks flourish
Is Science Necessary? Essays on Science and Scientists

Scientists like myself merely use their gifts to show up that which already exists, and we look small compared to the artists who create works of beauty out of themselves.
"Max F. Perutz - Banquet Speech". Nobelprize.org. 27 Nov 2012

A discovery is like falling in love and reaching the top of a mountain after a hard climb all in one, an ecstasy not induced by drugs but by the revelation of a face of nature that no one has seen before and that often turns out to be more subtle and wonderful than anyone had imagined.
'True Science', review of Peter Medawar, Advice to a Young Scientist (1980). In The London Review of Books (Mar 1981), 6.

For Christmas, 1939, a girl friend gave me a book token which I used to buy Linus Pauling's recently published Nature of the Chemical Bond. His book transformed the chemical flatland of my earlier textbooks into a world of three-dimensional structures.
'What Holds Molecules Together', in I Wish I'd Made You Angry Earlier (1998), 165.

I rarely plan my research; it plans me.
'My Commonplace Book', in I Wish I'd Made You Angry Earlier (1998), 314.

On hearing the news [of being awarded a Nobel Prize], a friend who knows me only too well, sent me this laconic message: 'Blood, toil, sweat and tears always were a good mixture'.
Nobel Banquet Speech (10 Dec 1962).

Scientists like myself merely use their gifts to show up that which already exists, and we look small compared to the artists who create works of beauty out of themselves. If a good fairy came and offered me back my youth, asking me which gifts I would rather have, those to make visible a thing which exists but which no man has ever seen before, or the genius needed to create, in a style of architecture never imagined before, the great Town Hall in which we are dining tonight, I might be tempted to choose the latter.
Nobel Banquet Speech (10 Dec 1962).

What is known for certain is dull.
'My Commonplace Book', in I Wish I'd Made You Angry Earlier (1998), 314.

When I saw the alpha-helix and saw what a beautiful, elegant structure it was, I was thunderstruck and was furious with myself for not having built this, but on the other hand, I wondered, was it really right?So I cycled home for lunch and was so preoccupied with the turmoil in my mind that didn't respond to anything. Then I had an idea, so I cycled back to the lab. I realized that I had a horse hair in a drawer. I set it up on the X-ray camera and gave it a two hour exposure, then took the film to the dark room with my heart in my mouth, wondering what it showed, and when I developed it, there was the 1.5 angstrom reflection which I had predicted and which excluded all structures other than the alpha-helix.So on Monday morning I stormed into my professor's office, into Bragg's office and showed him this, and Bragg said, 'Whatever made you think of that?' And I said, 'Because I was so furious with myself for having missed that beautiful structure.' To which Bragg replied coldly, 'I wish I had made you angry earlier.'
From transcript of audio of Max Perutz in BBC programme, 'Lifestory: Linus Pauling' (1997). On 'Linus Pauling and the Race for DNA' webpage 'I Wish I Had Made You Angry Earlier.'

Women's liberation could have not succeeded if science had not provided them with contraception and household technology.
'The Impact of Science on Society: The Challenge for Education', in J. L. Lewis and P. J. Kelly (eds.), Science and Technology and Future Human Needs (1987), 18.

Roald Hoffmann

Prize Motivation: "*for their theories, developed independently, concerning the course of chemical reactions*"
Prize Year: *1981*
Prize Category: *Chemistry*
Source: *nobelprize.org*

...chemists make molecules, by hard work, clever construction, and chance. They create, subject to some governing rules, something new, often something that has not been on Earth before. And then they study their creation, see its properties and relationships. They contemplate it. And they go on to make more molecules. I think the process is much like art. But there are differences.
When asked about "Becoming a Chemist - You are a theoretical chemist. Who inspired your love for organic chemistry? Why does "Making Molecules" put chemistry very close to the arts?"

Liberato Cardellini, "Looking for Connections: an Interview with Roald Hoffmann," Journal of Chemical Education 84(10), 1631-1635 (2007)

Science is a social system of Western European invention, not an American one, for gaining reliable knowledge, I would say not truth...
"Roald Hoffmann Interview". Nobelprize.org. 27 Nov 2012

I love chemistry because it's sort of human in scale - infinitely complex, but always tangible, always real.
Malcolm Browne, "Seeking Beauty in Atoms", The New York Times (1993)

The beautiful in nature has to do with the form of the object, which consists in the boundary. The sublime, on the other hand, is to be found in a formless object, insofar as in it or by occasion of it boundlessness is represented, and yet its totality is also present to thought."
Beyond the Finite: The Sublime in Art and Science by Iain Boyd Whyte, Roald Hoffmann

We feel ourselves elevated because we identify ourselves with the powers of nature, ascribing their vast impact to ourselves, because our fantasy rests on the wings of the storm as we roar into the heights and wander into the depths of infinity. Thus we ourselves expand into a boundless natural power.
Beyond the Finite: The Sublime in Art and Science by Iain Boyd Whyte, Roald Hoffmann

This is the paradox of the sublime. The gap between tangible, empirical objects, on one hand, and the world of the supersensible, on the other, is absolute and unbridgeable. Yet only through our failure to represent the supersensible can we have a presentiment of its existence. In this very ambivalence lies the power of the sublime.
Beyond the Finite:The Sublime in Art and Science by Iain Boyd Whyte, Roald Hoffmann

The gap between tangible, empirical objects, on one hand, and the world of the supersensible, on the other, is absolute and unbridgeable.
Beyond the Finite:The Sublime in Art and Science by Iain Boyd Whyte, Roald Hoffmann

Dismissing as reductive and one-dimensional the modernist conception of the human condition as rational, progressive, and benign, the postmodern critique found in the sublime a device for exploring more profound and complex layers of meaning: the heroic, the mysterious, and the numinous.
Beyond the Finite:The Sublime in Art and Science by Iain Boyd Whyte, Roald Hoffmann

Once we had discovered cooking, that allowed our cranial plates to expand (i.e., no longer constricted by massive masseter muscles needed to grind our food), cortical expansion was based on a multiplication of "computer chip"-like repetitive structures of three thousand neurons or so-called cortical columns.
Beyond the Finite:The Sublime in Art and Science by Iain Boyd Whyte, Roald Hoffmann

Music, perhaps better than any other art form, reflects our deep social-emotional nature.
Beyond the Finite:The Sublime in Art and Science by Iain Boyd Whyte, Roald Hoffmann

John C. Polanyi

Prize Motivation: "*for their contributions concerning the dynamics of chemical elementary processes*"
Prize Year: *1986*
Prize Category: *Chemistry*
Source: nobelprize.org

Authority in science exists to be questioned, since heresy is the spring from which new ideas flow.

Idealism is the highest form of reason.

In science, truth must take precedence not only over individual advantage, but also over 'group advantage' – sectional interests such as nationality, creed or ethnicity.
"John C. Polanyi - On Being a Scientist: A Personal View". Nobelprize.org. 27 Nov 2012

Science never gives up searching for truth, since it never claims to have achieved it. It is civilizing because it puts truth ahead of all else, including personal interests.
"John C. Polanyi - On Being a Scientist: A Personal View". Nobelprize.org. 27 Nov 2012

Faced with the admitted difficulty of managing the creative process, we are doubling our efforts to do so. Is this because science has failed to deliver, having given us nothing more than nuclear power, penicillin, space travel, genetic engineering, transistors, and superconductors? Or is it because governments everywhere regard as a reproach activities they cannot advantageously control? They felt that way about the marketplace for goods, but trillions of wasted dollars later, they have come to recognize the efficiency of this self-regulating system. Not so, however, with the marketplace for ideas.
Quoted in Martin Moskovits (ed.), Science and Society, the John C. Polanyi Nobel Lareates Lectures (1995), 8.

I knew, however, that it would cost ten times what I had available in order to build a molecular beam machine. I decided to follow a byway, rather than the highway. It is a procedure I have subsequently recommended to beginning scientists in this country, where research strategy is best modelled on that used by Wolfe at the Plains of Abraham.(British General James Wolfe defeated the French defending Quebec in 1759 after scaling a cliff for a surprise attack.)
'A Scientist and the World He Lives In', Speech to the Empire Club of

Canada (27 Nov 1986) in C. Frank Turner and Tim Dickson (eds.), The Empire Club of Canada Speeches 1986-1987 (1987), 149-161.

It is folly to use as one's guide in the selection of fundamental science the criterion of utility. Not because (scientists)... despise utility. But because. .. useful outcomes are best identified after the making of discoveries, rather than before.Concerning the allocation of research funds.
Speech to the Canadian Society for the Weizmann Institute of Science, Toronto (2 Jun 1996)

It takes a trained and discerning researcher to keep the goal in sight, and to detect evidence of the creeping progress toward it.
from a speech to the Empire Club of Canada (27 Nov 1986)

Nothing is more irredeemably irrelevant than bad science.
quoted in H. W. Wilson Co., Nobel Prize Winners (1987)

Science is an enterprise that can only flourish if it puts the truth ahead of nationality, ethnicity, class and color.
from a speech at the University of California at Berkeley (1994) quoted in Encyclopedia of World Biography, 2nd ed., Gale Research, (1998)

[Intellectual courage is] the quality that allows one to believe in one's judgement in the face of disappointment and widespread skepticism. Intellectual courage is even rarer than physical courage.
'A Scientist and the World He Lives In', Speech to the Empire Club of Canada (27 Nov 1986) in C. Frank Turner and Tim Dickson (eds.), The Empire Club of Canada Speeches 1986-1987 (1987), 149-161.

Kary B. Mullis

Prize Motivation: "*for his invention of the polymerase chain reaction (PCR) method*"
Prize Year: *1993*
Prize Category: *Chemistry*
Source: *nobelprize.org*

Each of us have things and thoughts and descriptions of an amazing universe in our possession that kings in the 17th Century would have gone to war to possess.

For a reaction with the potential which I dreamed of for this one, especially in light of the absence of anything else that could do the same thing, time was only a very secondary consideration. Would it work at all was important. The next most important thing was, would it be easy to do? Then came time.
Kary B. Mullis - Nobel Lecture: The Polymerase Chain Reaction". Nobelprize.org. 27 Nov 2012

This was typical of a chemist; chemists always believe they're smarter than biochemists. Of course, physicists think they're smarter than chemists, mathematicians think they're smarter than physicists, and, for a while, philosophers thought they were smarter than mathematicians, until they found out in this century that they really didn't have anything much to talk about.
Dancing Naked in the Mind Field by Kary Mullis

This is what happens when government agencies, who have to answer to nobody in particular, run rampant. If you want to have sodium chloride in your lab, you must have safety equipment that would be appropriate for sodium metal and chlorine gas. If you want to have it in a restaurant, you just have to have a salt shaker.
Dancing Naked in the Mind Field by Kary Mullis

The appropriate demeanor for a human is to feel lucky that he is alive and to humble himself in the face of the immensity of things and have a beer. Relax. Welcome to Earth. It's a little confusing at first. That's why you have to come back over and over again before you learn to really enjoy yourself.
Dancing Naked in the Mind Field by Kary Mullis

we have this inaccurate perception that everything that is real is perceptible by at least one of our senses, and invisible things are kind of freaky.
Dancing Naked in the Mind Field by Kary Mullis

for any human interaction to work both parties must believe they are getting the better deal.
Dancing Naked in the Mind Field by Kary Mullis

Nobody who is sane understands what goes on down at the level where the fundamental things like quarks and electrons do not have any volume or any position. If you can understand something with zero volume and no position, then welcome to insanity.
Dancing Naked in the Mind Field by Kary Mullis

It doesn't take a lot of education to check things out. All it takes is access to resources and a minor distrust of everyone else on the planet and a feeling that they may be trying to put something over on you.
Dancing Naked in the Mind Field by Kary Mullis

There is a general place in your brain, I think, reserved for "melancholy of relationships past." It grows and prospers as life progresses, forcing you finally, against your better judgment, to listen to country music.
Dancing Naked in the Mind Field by Kary Mullis Kary B. Mullis - Nobel Lecture: The Polymerase Chain Reaction". Nobelprize.org. 27 Nov 2012

Physics Nobel Laureates

Marie Curie, née Sklodowska

Prize Motivation: "*in recognition of the extraordinary services they have rendered by their joint researches on the radiation phenomena discovered by Professor Henri Becquerel*"
Prize Year: *1903*
Prize Category: *Physics*
Source: nobelprize.org

I am one of those who think like Nobel, that humanity will draw more good than evil from new discoveries.
As quoted in White Coat Tales : Medicine's Heroes, Heritage and Misadventures (2007) by Robert B. Taylor, p. 141

I was taught that the way of progress was neither swift nor easy.
Java Connector Architecture : Building Custom Connectors and Adapters (2002) by Atul Apte, p. 69

Humanity needs practical men, who get the most out of their work, and, without forgetting the general good, safeguard their own interests. But humanity also needs dreamers, for whom the disinterested development of an enterprise is so captivating that it becomes impossible for them to devote their care to their own material profit. Without doubt, these dreamers do not deserve wealth, because they do not desire it. Even so, a well-organized society should assure to such workers the efficient means of accomplishing their task, in a life freed from material care and freely consecrated to research.
As quoted in Astrophysics of the Diffuse Universe (2003) by Michael A. Dopita and Ralph S. Sutherland

Nothing in life is to be feared, it is only to be understood. Now is the time to understand more, so that we may fear less.
As quoted in Our Precarious Habitat (1973) by Melvin A. Benarde, p. v

I am among those who think that science has great beauty. A scientist in his laboratory is not only a technician: he is also a child placed before natural phenomena which impress him like a fairy tale. We should not allow it to be believed that all scientific progress can be reduced to mechanisms, machines, gearings, even though such machinery also has its beauty. Neither do I believe that the spirit of adventure runs any risk of disappearing in our world. If I see anything vital around me, it is precisely that spirit of adventure, which seems indestructible and is akin to curiosity.
As quoted in Madame Curie : A Biography (1937) by Eve Curie Labouisse, as translated by Vincent Sheean, p. 341

I believe international work is a heavy task, but that it is nevertheless indispensable to go through an apprenticeship in it, at the cost of many efforts and also of a real spirit of sacrifice: however imperfect it may be, the work of Geneva has a grandeur that deserves our support.
Letter to Eve Curie (July 1929), as quoted in Madame Curie : A Biography (1937) by Eve Curie Labouisse, as translated by Vincent Sheean, p. 341

You cannot hope to build a better world without improving the individuals. To that end each of us must work for his own improvement, and at the same time share a general responsibility for all humanity, our particular duty being to aid those to whom we think we can be most useful.
Pierre Curie (1923), as translated by Charlotte Kellogg and Vernon Lyman Kellogg, p. 168

All my life through, the new sights of Nature made me rejoice like a child.
Pierre Curie (1923), as translated by Charlotte Kellogg and Vernon Lyman Kellogg, p. 162

We must not forget that when radium was discovered no one knew that it would prove useful in hospitals. The work was one of pure science. And this is a proof that scientific work must not be considered from the point of view of the direct usefulness of it. It must be done for itself, for the beauty of science, and then there is always the chance that a scientific discovery may become like the radium a benefit for humanity.
Lecture at Vassar College, Poughkeepsie, New York (14 May 1921)

Be less curious about people and more curious about ideas.
Response to a reporter seeking an interview during a vacation with her husband in Brittany, who mistaking her for a housekeeper, asked her if there was anything confidential she could recount, as quoted in Living Adventures in Science (1972), by Henry Thomas and Dana Lee Thomas Variant: In science, we must be interested in things, not in persons.

One never notices what has been done; one can only see what remains to be done.
Letter to her brother (1894)

Max Karl Ernst Ludwig Planck

 **Prize Motivation:** "*in recognition of the services he rendered to the advancement of Physics by his discovery of energy quanta*"
Prize Year: *1918*
Prize Category: *Physics*
Source: nobelprize.org

The assumption of an absolute determinism is the essential foundation of every scientific enquiry.
Physikalische Abhandlungen und Vorträge (1958), Vol 3, 89. Translated in J. L. Heilbron, The Dilemmas of an Upright Man (1986) 66.

A scientist is happy, not in resting on his attainments but in the steady acquisition of fresh knowledge.
The Philosophy of Physics. Collected in The New Science: 3 Complete Works (1959), 253.

The entire world we apprehend through our senses is no more than a tiny fragment in the vastness of Nature.
The Universe in the Light of Modern Physics (1931), 8.

An important scientific innovation rarely makes its way by gradually winning over and converting its opponents. What does happen is that its opponents gradually die out, and that the growing generation is familiarized with the ideas from the beginning.
Scientific Autobiography and Other Papers, trans. F. Gaynor (1950), 97. Quoted in David L. Hull, Science as a Process (1990), 379.

The goal is nothing other than the coherence and completeness of the system not only in respect of all details, but also in respect of all physicists of all places, all times, all peoples, and all cultures.
Acht Vorlesungen (1910), 'Vorwort': 4. Translated in J. L. Heilbron, The Dilemmas of an Upright Man (1986), 51.

Anybody who has been seriously engaged in scientific work of any kind realizes that over the entrance to the gates of the temple of science are written the words: Ye must have faith. It is a quality which the scientist cannot dispense with.
Where is Science Going?, translated by James Vincent Murphy (1932), 214.

The whole strenuous intellectual work of an industrious research worker would appear, after all, in vain and hopeless, if he were not occasionally through some striking facts to find that he had, at the end of all his criss-cross journeys, at last accomplished at least one step which was conclusively nearer the truth.
Nobel Lecture (2 Jun 1920), in Nobel Lectures in Physics, 1901-1921 (1998), 407.

Both religion and natural science require a belief in God for their activities, to the former He is the starting point, and to the latter the goal of every thought process. To the former He is the foundation, to the latter, the crown of the edifice of every generalized world view.
Lecture, 'Religion and Natural Science' (1937) In Max Planck and Frank Gaynor (trans.), Scientific Autobiography and Other Papers (1949), 184.

This is one of man's oldest riddles. How can the independence of human volition be harmonized with the fact that we are integral parts of a universe which is subject to the rigid order of nature's laws?
In Where is Science Going? (1932), 107.

Experimenters are the shock troops of science.
'The Meaning and Limits of Exact Science', Science (30 Sep 1949), 110, No. 2857, 325. Advance reprinting of chapter from book Max Planck, Scientific Autobiography (1949), 110.

When I began my physical studies [in Munich in 1874] and sought advice from my venerable teacher Philipp von Jolly...he portrayed to me physics as a highly developed, almost fully matured science...Possibly in one or another nook there would perhaps be a dust particle or a small bubble to be examined and classified, but the system as a whole stood there fairly secured, and theoretical physics approached visibly that degree of perfection which, for example, geometry has had already for centuries.
From a lecture (1924). In Damien Broderick (ed.), Year Million: Science at the Far Edge of Knowledge (2008), 104.

I had always looked upon the search for the absolute as the noblest and most worth while task of science.
'A Scientific Autobiography' (1948), in Scientific Autobiography and Other Papers, trans. Frank Gaynor (1950), 46.

I regard consciousness as fundamental. I regard matter as derivative from consciousness. We cannot get behind consciousness. Everything that we talk about, everything that we regard as existing, postulates consciousness.
Quoted in The Observer (25 Jan 1931). Cited in Joseph H. Fussell, 'Where is Science Going?: Review and Comment', Theosophical Path Magazine, January to December 1933 (2003), 199.

It is not the possession of truth, but the success which attends the seeking after it, that enriches the seeker and brings happiness to him.
In Where is Science Going? (1932), 200.

My original decision to devote myself to science was a direct result of the discovery which has never ceased to fill me with enthusiasm since my early youth—the comprehension of the far from obvious fact that the laws of human reasoning coincide with the laws governing the sequences of the impressions we receive from the world about us; that, therefore, pure reasoning can enable man to gain an insight into the mechanism of the latter. In this connection, it is of paramount importance that the outside world is something independent from man, something absolute, and the quest for the laws which apply to this absolute appeared to me as the most sublime scientific pursuit in life.
'A Scientific Autobiography' (1948), in Scientific Autobiography and Other Papers, trans. Frank Gaynor (1950), 13.

New scientific ideas never spring from a communal body, however organized, but rather from the head of an individually inspired researcher who struggles with his problems in lonely thought and unites all his thought on one single point which is his whole world for the moment.
Address on the 25th anniversary of the Kaiser-Wilhelm Gesellschaft (Jan 1936). Quoted in Surviving the Swastika: Scientific Research in Nazi Germany (1993), 97.

Physical changes take place continuously, while chemical changes take place discontinuously. Physics deals chiefly with continuous varying quantities, while chemistry deals chiefly with whole numbers.
Treatise on Thermodynamics (1897), trans. Alexander Ogg (1903), 22, footnote.

Religion belongs to the realm that is inviolable before the law of causation and therefore closed to science.
Where is Science Going?, (1932). Collected in The New Science (1959), 121.

Science cannot solve the ultimate mystery of nature. And that is because, in the last analysis, we ourselves are part of nature and therefore part of the mystery that we are trying to solve.
Where is Science Going?, trans. James Murphy (1933), Epilogue, 217.

Science enhances the moral value of life, because it furthers a love of truth and reverence—love of truth displaying itself in the constant endeavor to arrive at a more exact knowledge of the world of mind and matter around us, and reverence, because every advance in knowledge brings us face to face with the mystery of our own being.
In Where is Science Going? (1932), 169.

Scientific discovery and scientific knowledge have been achieved only by those who have gone in pursuit of them without any practical purpose whatsoever in view.
The New Science (1959), 93.

Albert Einstein

Prize Motivation: "*for his services to Theoretical Physics, and especially for his discovery of the law of the photoelectric effect*'
Prize Year: *1921*
Prize Category: *Physics*
Source: *nobelprize.org*

Great spirits have always encountered violent opposition from mediocre minds. The mediocre mind is incapable of understanding the man who refuses to bow blindly to conventional prejudices and chooses instead to express his opinions courageously and honestly.
Letter to Morris Raphael Cohen, professor emeritus of philosophy at the College of the City of New York, defending the appointment of Bertrand Russell to a teaching position (19 March 1940).

Today the atomic bomb has altered profoundly the nature of the world as we know it, and the human race consequently finds itself in a new habitat to which it must adapt its thinking... Never before was it possible for one nation to make war on another without sending armies across borders. Now with rockets and atomic bombs no center of population on the earth's surface is secure from surprise destruction in a single attack... Few men have ever seen the bomb. But all men if told a few facts can understand that this bomb and the danger of war is a very real thing, and not something far away. It directly concerns every person in the civilized world. We cannot leave it to generals, senators, and diplomats to work out a solution over a period of generations... There is no defense in science against the weapon which can destroy civilization. Our defense is not in armaments, nor in science, nor in going underground. Our defense is in law and order... Future thinking must prevent wars
"Only Then Shall We Find Courage" (in an interview with Michael Amrine), published in the New York Times Magazine, June 23, 1946, and later in pamphlet form by the Emergency Committee of Atomic Scientists.

Imagination is more important than knowledge. For knowledge is limited, whereas imagination embraces the entire world, stimulating progress, giving birth to evolution. It is, strictly speaking, a real factor in scientific research.
Cosmic Religion : With Other Opinions and Aphorisms (1931) by Albert Einstein, p. 97

"Great spirits have always encountered violent opposition from mediocre minds."
Einstein's Cosmos: How Albert Einstein's Vision Transformed Our Understanding of Space and Time (Great Discoveries) by Michio Kaku

The most beautiful experience we can have is the mysterious. It is the fundamental emotion which stands at the cradle of true art and true science. Whoever does not know it and can no longer wonder, no longer marvel, is as good as dead, and his eyes are dimmed.
Ideas And Opinions by Albert Einstein

I do not know with what weapons World War III will be fought, but World War IV will be fought with sticks and stones.
Lost in Shangri-La: A True Story of Survival, Adventure, and the Most Incredible Rescue Mission of World War II (P.S.) by Mitchell Zuckoff As quoted in an interview with Alfred Werner, published in Liberal Judaism 16 (April-May 1949), 12. Einstein Archive 30-1104, as sourced in The New Quotable Einstein by Alice Calaprice (2005), p. 173.

Man should not have to work for the achievement of the necessities of life to such an extent that he has neither time nor strength for personal activities.
Out of My Later Years: The Scientist, Philosopher, and Man Portrayed Through His Own Words by Albert Einstein

I live in that solitude which is painful in youth, but delicious in the years of maturity.
Out of My Later Years: The Scientist, Philosopher, and Man Portrayed Through His Own Words by Albert Einstein

I am firmly convinced that the passionate will for justice and truth has done more to improve man's condition than calculating political shrewdness which in the long run only breeds general distrust.
Out of My Later Years: The Scientist, Philosopher, and Man Portrayed Through His Own Words by Albert Einstein

Education is that which remains, if one has forgotten everything he learned in school.
Out of My Later Years: The Scientist, Philosopher, and Man Portrayed Through His Own Words by Albert Einstein

The value of a man, however, should be seen in what he gives and not in what he is able to receive.
Out of My Later Years: The Scientist, Philosopher, and Man Portrayed Through His Own Words by Albert Einstein

We must not only tolerate differences between individuals and between groups, but we should indeed welcome them and look upon them as an enriching of our existence. That is the essence of all true tolerance; without tolerance in this widest sense there can be no question of true morality.
Out of My Later Years: The Scientist, Philosopher, and Man Portrayed Through His Own Words by Albert Einstein

All religions, arts and sciences are branches of the same tree. All these aspirations are directed toward ennobling man's life, lifting it from the sphere of mere physical existence and leading the individual toward freedom.
Out of My Later Years: The Scientist, Philosopher, and Man Portrayed Through His Own Words by Albert Einstein

The significant problems we face cannot be solved at the same level of thinking we were at when we created them.
The 7 Habits of Highly Effective People by Stephen R. Covey From "Atomic Education Urged by Einstein", New York Times (25 May 1946), and later quoted in the article "The Real Problem is in the Hearts of Man" by Michael Amrine, from the New York Times Magazine (23 June 1946)

The world is a dangerous place, not because of those who do evil, but because of those who look on and do nothing.
The Sociopath Next Door by Martha Stout Ph.D. Einstein's tribute to Pablo Casals (30 March 1953), in Conversations with Casals (1957), by Josep Maria Corredor, translated from Conversations avec Pablo Casals : souvenirs et opinions d'un musicien (1955).

The ideals which have lighted me on my way and time after time given me new courage to face life cheerfully, have been Truth, Goodness, and Beauty.
The World As I See It by Albert Einstein

The man who regards his own life and that of his fellow-creatures as meaningless is not merely unfortunate but almost disqualified for life.
The World As I See It by Albert Einstein

The really valuable thing in the pageant of human life seems to me not the State but the creative, sentient individual, the personality; it alone creates the noble and the sublime, while the herd as such remains dull in thought and dull in feeling.
The World As I See It by Albert Einstein

I cannot conceive of a God who rewards and punishes his creatures, or has a will of the type of which we are conscious in ourselves. An individual who should survive his physical death is also beyond my comprehension, nor do I wish it otherwise; such notions are for the fears or absurd egoism of feeble souls. Enough for me the mystery of the eternity of life, and the inkling of the marvellous structure of reality, together with the single-hearted endeavour to comprehend a portion, be it never so tiny, of the reason that manifests itself in nature.
The World As I See It by Albert Einstein

The true value of a human being is determined primarily by the measure and the sense in which he has attained to liberation from the self.
The World As I See It by Albert Einstein

Niels Henrik David Bohr

Prize Motivation: "*for his services in the investigation of the structure of atoms and of the radiation emanating from them*"
Prize Year: *1922*
Prize Category: *Physics*
Source: nobelprize.org

It is not enough to be wrong, one must also be polite.
As quoted in The Genius of Science: A Portrait Gallery (2000) by Abraham Pais, p. 24

How wonderful that we have met with a paradox. Now we have some hope of making progress.
As quoted in Niels Bohr : The Man, His Science, & the World They Changed (1966) by Ruth Moore, p. 196

Every valuable human being must be a radical and a rebel, for what he must aim at is to make things better than they are.
As quoted in The World of the Atom;; (1966) by Henry Abraham Boorse and Lloyd Motz, p. 741

There is no quantum world. There is only an abstract physical description. It is wrong to think that the task of physics is to find out how nature is. Physics concerns what we can say about nature...
As quoted in "The philosophy of Niels Bohr" by Aage Petersen, in the Bulletin of the Atomic Scientists Vol. 19, No. 7 (September 1963); The Genius of Science: A Portrait Gallery (2000) by Abraham Pais, p. 24, and Niels Bohr: Reflections on Subject and Object (2001) by Paul. McEvoy, p. 291

Physics is to be regarded not so much as the study of something a priori given, but rather as the development of methods of ordering and surveying human experience. In this respect our task must be to account for such experience in a manner independent of individual subjective judgement and therefore objective in the sense that it can be unambiguously communicated in ordinary human language.
"The Unity of Human Knowledge" (October 1960)

We are all agreed that your theory is crazy. The question that divides us is whether it is crazy enough to have a chance of being correct.
Said to Wolfgang Pauli after his presentation of Heisenberg's and Pauli's nonlinear field theory of elementary particles, at Columbia University (1958), as quoted in Symposium on Basic Research (1959) by Dael Lee Wolfle, p. 66

An expert is a person who has found out by his own painful experience all the mistakes that one can make in a very narrow field.

As quoted by Edward Teller, in Dr. Edward Teller's Magnificent Obsession by Robert Coughlan, in LIFE magazine (6 September 1954), p. 62

For a parallel to the lesson of atomic theory regarding the limited applicability of such customary idealizations, we must in fact turn to quite other branches of science, such as psychology, or even to that kind of epistemological problems with which already thinkers like Buddha and Lao Tzu have been confronted, when trying to harmonize our position as spectators and actors in the great drama of existence.

Speech on quantum theory at Celebrazione del Secondo Centenario della Nascita di Luigi Galvani, Bologna, Italy (October 1937)

What is it that we humans depend on? We depend on our words... Our task is to communicate experience and ideas to others. We must strive continually to extend the scope of our description, but in such a way that our messages do not thereby lose their objective or unambiguous character ... We are suspended in language in such a way that we cannot say what is up and what is down. The word "reality" is also a word, a word which we must learn to use correctly.

Quoted in Philosophy of Science Vol. 37 (1934), p. 157, and in The Truth of Science : Physical Theories and Reality (1997) by Roger Gerhard Newton, p. 176

We must be clear that when it comes to atoms, language can be used only as in poetry. The poet, too, is not nearly so concerned with describing facts as with creating images and establishing mental connections.

"Atomic Physics and the Description of Nature" (1934)

Truth is something that we can attempt to doubt, and then perhaps, after much exertion, discover that part of the doubt is not justified.

Quoted in Bill Becker, 'Pioneer of the Atom', New York Times Sunday Magazine (20 Oct 1957), 52.

Werner Karl Heisenberg

Prize Motivation: "*for the creation of quantum mechanics, the application of which has, inter alia, led to the discovery of the allotropic forms of hydrogen*"
Prize Year: *1932*
Prize Category: *Physics*
Source: nobelprize.org

We have to remember that what we observe is not nature herself, but nature exposed to our method of questioning.
Physics and Philosophy: The Revolution in Modern Science (1958) Lectures delivered at University of St. Andrews, Scotland, Winter 1955-56

The physicist may be satisfied when he has the mathematical scheme and knows how to use for the interpretation of the experiments. But he has to speak about his results also to non-physicists who will not be satisfied unless some explanation is given in plain language. Even for the physicist the description in plain language will be the criterion of the degree of understanding that has been reached.
Physics and Philosophy: The Revolution in Modern Science (1958) Lectures delivered at University of St. Andrews, Scotland, Winter 1955-56

Whenever we proceed from the known into the unknown we may hope to understand, but we may have to learn at the same time a new meaning of the word "understanding."
Physics and Philosophy: The Revolution in Modern Science (1958) Lectures delivered at University of St. Andrews, Scotland, Winter 1955-56

The existing scientific concepts cover always only a very limited part of reality, and the other part that has not yet been understood is infinite.
Physics and Philosophy: The Revolution in Modern Science (1958) Lectures delivered at University of St. Andrews, Scotland, Winter 1955-56

There is a fundamental error in separating the parts from the whole, the mistake of atomizing what should not be atomized. Unity and complementarity constitute reality.
As quoted in Physics from Wholeness : Dynamical Totality as a Conceptual Foundation for Physical Theories (2005) by Barbara Piechocinska The smallest units of matter are not physical objects in the ordinary sense; they are forms, ideas which can be expressed unambiguously only in mathematical language.

In general, scientific progress calls for no more than the absorption and elaboration of new ideas— and this is a call most scientists are happy to heed.
Physics and Beyond : Encounters and Conversation (1971)

Quantum theory provides us with a striking illustration of the fact that we can fully understand a connection though we can only speak of it in images and parables.
Physics and Beyond : Encounters and Conversation (1971)

An expert is someone who knows some of the worst mistakes that can be made in his subject, and how to avoid them.
Physics and Beyond : Encounters and Conversation (1971)

Every experiment destroys some of the knowledge of the system which was obtained by previous experiments.
"Critique of the Physical Concepts of the Corpuscular Theory" in The Physical Principles of the Quantum Theory (1930) as translated by Carl Eckhart and Frank C. Hoyt, p. 20; also in "The Uncertainty Principle" in The World of Mathematics : A Small Library of the Literature of Mathematics (1956) by James Roy Newman, p. 1051

Light and matter are both single entities, and the apparent duality arises in the limitations of our language. It is not surprising that our language should be incapable of describing the processes occurring within the atoms, for, as has been remarked, it was invented to describe the experiences of daily life, and these consist only of processes involving exceedingly large numbers of atoms. Furthermore, it is very difficult to modify our language so that it will be able to describe these atomic processes, for words can only describe things of which we can form mental pictures, and this ability, too, is a result of daily experience. Fortunately, mathematics is not subject to this limitation, and it has been possible to invent a mathematical scheme — the quantum theory — which seems entirely adequate for the treatment of atomic processes; for visualisation, however, we must content ourselves with two incomplete analogies — the wave picture and the corpuscular picture.
"Introductory" in The Physical Principles of the Quantum Theory (1930) as translated by Carl Eckhart and Frank C. Hoyt, p. 10

Paul Adrien Maurice Dirac

Prize Motivation: "*for the discovery of new productive forms of atomic theory*"
Prize Year: *1933*
Prize Category: *Physics*
Source: nobelprize.org

If you are receptive and humble, mathematics will lead you by the hand. Again and again, when I have been at a loss how to proceed, I have just had to wait until I have felt the mathematics lead me by the hand. It has lead me along an unexpected path, a path where new vistas open up, a path leading to new territory, where one can set up a base of operations, from which one can survey the surroundings and plan future progress.
As quoted in The Strangest Man: The Hidden Life of Paul Dirac, Mystic of the Atom (2009) by Graham Farmelo, p. 435

In science one tries to tell people, in such a way as to be understood by everyone, something that no one ever knew before. But in the case of poetry, it's the exact opposite!
As quoted in Brighter Than a Thousand Suns : A Personal History of the Atomic Scientists (1958) by Robert Jungk, as translated by James Cleugh, p. 22 Anecdotally, when Oppenheimer was working at Göttingen, Dirac supposedly came to him one day and said: "Oppenheimer, they tell me you are writing poetry. I do not see how a man can work on the frontiers of physics and write poetry at the same time. They are in opposition. In science you want to say something that nobody knew before, in words which everyone can understand. In poetry you are bound to say... something that everybody knows already in words that nobody can understand."

There is in my opinion a great similarity between the problems provided by the mysterious behavior of the atom and those provided by the present economic paradoxes confronting the world. In both cases one is given a great many facts which are expressible with numbers, and one has to find the underlying principles. The methods of theoretical physics should be applicable to all those branches of thought in which the essential features are expressible with numbers.
"Paul A.M. Dirac - Banquet Speech". Nobelprize.org. 15 Nov 2012

A good deal of my research in physics has consisted in not setting out to solve some particular problem, but simply examining mathematical equations of a kind that physicists use and trying to fit them together in an interesting way, regardless of any application that the work may have. It is simply a search for pretty mathematics. It may turn out later to have an application. Then one has good luck. At age 78.

International Journal of Theoretical Physics (1982), 21, 603. In A. Pais, 'Playing With Equations, the Dirac Way'. Behram N. Kursunoglu (Ed.) and Eugene Paul Wigner (Ed.), Paul Adrien Maurice Dirac: Reminiscences about a Great Physicist (1990), 110.

As time goes on, it becomes increasingly evident that the rules which the mathematician finds interesting are the same as those which Nature has chosen.At age 36.

"Proceedings of the Royal Society of Edinburgh (1939), 59 122. In A. Pais, 'Playing With Equations, the Dirac Way'. Behram N. Kursunoglu (Ed.) and Eugene Paul Wigner (Ed.), Paul Adrien Maurice Dirac: Reminiscences about a Great Physicist (1990), 109.

God used beautiful mathematics in creating the world.

Quoted in Behram Kursunoglu and Eugene Paul Wigner, Paul Adrien Maurice Dirac (1990), Preface, xv.

Hopes are always accompanied by fears, and, in scientific research, the fears are liable to become dominant.At age 67.

Eureka (Oct 1969), No.32, 2-4.

I admired Bohr very much. We had long talks together, long talks in which Bohr did practically all the talking.Recalling his Sep 1926-Feb 1927 stay in Copenhagen.

In History of Twentieth Century Physics (1977), 109. In A. Pais, 'Playing With Equations, the Dirac Way'. Behram N. Kursunoglu (Ed.) and Eugene Paul Wigner (Ed.), Paul Adrien Maurice Dirac: Reminiscences about a Great Physicist (1990), 94.

I found the best ideas usually came, not when one was actively striving for them, but when one was in a more relaxed state... I used to take long solitary walks on Sundays, during which I tended to review the current situation in a leisurely way. Such occasions often proved fruitful, even though (or perhaps, because) the primary purpose of the walk was relaxation and not research.

'Methods in Theoretical Physics', From A Life of Physics: Evening Lectures at the International Centre for Theoretical Physics, Trieste, Italy. A Special Supplement of the IAEA Bulletin (1968), 24.

I think it is the general rule that the originator of a new idea is not the most suitable person to develop it, because his fears of something going wrong are really too strong...At age 69.

The Development of Quantum Theory (1971). In A. Pais, 'Playing With Equations, the Dirac Way'. Behram N. Kursunoglu (Ed.) and Eugene Paul Wigner (Ed.), Paul Adrien Maurice Dirac: Reminiscences about a Great Physicist (1990), 111.

It is more important to have beauty in one's equations than to have them fit experiment... It seems that if one is working from the point of view of getting beauty in one's equations, and if one has really a sound insight, one is on a sure line of progress. If there is not complete agreement between the results of one's work and experiment, one should not allow oneself to be too discouraged, because the discrepancy may well be due to minor features that are not properly taken into account and that will get cleared up with further developments of the theory.
'The Evolution of the Physicist's Picture of Nature', Scientific American, May 1963, 208, 47.

Pick a flower on Earth and you move the farthest star.
Attributed. In Benjamin Crowell, Newtonian Physics (2000), 193.

The mathematician plays a game in which he himself invents the rules while the physicist plays a game in which the rules are provided by nature, but as time goes on it becomes increasingly evident that the rules which the mathematician finds interesting are the same as those which nature has chosen.
In Ian Stewart, Why Beauty is Truth (2007), 279.

Well, in the first place, it leads to great anxiety as to whether it's going to be correct or not ... I expect that's the dominating feeling. It gets to be rather a fever...At age 60, when asked about his feelings on discovering the Dirac equation.
"Interview with T. Kuhn (7 May 1963), Niels Bohr Library, American Intitute of Physics, New York. In A. Pais, 'Playing With Equations, the Dirac Way'. Behram N. Kursunoglu (Ed.) and Eugene Paul Wigner (Ed.), Paul Adrien Maurice Dirac: Reminiscences about a Great Physicist (1990), 110.

In my case this article of faith is that the human race will continue to live for ever and will develop and progress without limit. This is an assumption that I must make for my peace of mind. Living is worthwhile if one can contribute in some small way to this endless chain of progress.
The Strangest Man: The Hidden Life of Paul Dirac, Mystic of the Atom by Graham Farmelo

The beauty of a fundamental theory in physics has several characteristics in common with a great work of art: fundamental simplicity, inevitability, power and grandeur. Like every great work of art, a beautiful theory in physics is always ambitious, never trifling.
The Strangest Man: The Hidden Life of Paul Dirac, Mystic of the Atom by Graham Farmelo

'Good prose is like a window pane.'59
The Strangest Man: The Hidden Life of Paul Dirac, Mystic of the Atom by Graham Farmelo

if everyone in the world spent twelve hours a day placing individual atoms into a thimble, a century would elapse before it was filled.
The Strangest Man: The Hidden Life of Paul Dirac, Quantum Genius by Graham Farmelo

'There are always more people who prefer to speak than to listen.'
The Strangest Man: The Hidden Life of Paul Dirac, Quantum Genius by Graham Farmelo

'I don't understand the equation on the top-right-hand corner of the blackboard.' Dirac says nothing. The audience shuffles nervously, but he remains silent, whiling away the time of day, looking unconcerned. The moderator, feeling obliged to break the silence, asks for a reply, whereupon Dirac says, 'That was not a question, it was a comment.'
The Strangest Man: The Hidden Life of Paul Dirac, Quantum Genius by Graham Farmelo

Erwin Schrödinger

Prize Motivation: "*for the discovery of new productive forms of atomic theory*"
Prize Year: *1933*
Prize Category: *Physics*
Source: nobelprize.org

If you cannot, in the long run, tell everyone what you have been doing, your doing has been worthless.
Attributed.

Science is a game—but a game with reality, a game with sharpened knives ... If a man cuts a picture carefully into 1000 pieces, you solve the puzzle when you reassemble the pieces into a picture; in the success or failure, both your intelligences compete. In the presentation of a scientific problem, the other player is the good Lord. He has not only set the problem but also has devised the rules of the game, but they are not completely known, half of them are left for you to discover or to deduce. The experiment is the tempered blade which you wield with success against the spirits of darkness—or which defeats you shamefully. The uncertainty is how many of the rules God himself has permanently ordained, and how many apparently are caused by your own mental inertia, while the solution generally becomes possible only through freedom from its limitations.
Quoted in Walter Moore, Schrödinger: Life and Thought (1989), 348.

The task is ... not so much to see what no one has yet seen; but to think what nobody has yet thought, about that which everybody sees.
Quoted in L. Bertalanffy, Problems of Life (1952).

Why are atoms so small? ... Many examples have been devised to bring this fact home to an audience, none of them more impressive than the one used by Lord Kelvin: Suppose that you could mark the molecules in a glass of water, then pour the contents of the glass into the ocean and stir the latter thoroughly so as to distribute the marked molecules uniformly throughout the seven seas; if you then took a glass of water anywhere out of the ocean, you would find in it about a hundred of your marked molecules.
What is life?: the Physical Aspect of the Living Cell (1944). Collected in What is Life? with Mind And Matter & Autobiographical Sketches (1967, 1992), 6-7.

"What we cannot comprehend within space and time," the physicist Erwin Schrödinger observed, "we cannot comprehend at all."
One, Two, Three: Absolutely Elementary Mathematics by David Berlinski

How can the events in space and time which take place within the spatial boundary of a living organism be accounted for by physics and chemistry?
What Is Life?: with "Mind and Matter" and "Autobiographical Sketches" by Erwin Schrödinger, Roger Penrose

Only in the co-operation of an enormously large number of atoms do statistical laws begin to operate and control the behaviour of these assemblies with an accuracy increasing as the number of atoms involved increases. It is in that way that the events acquire truly orderly features.
What Is Life?: with "Mind and Matter" and "Autobiographical Sketches" by Erwin Schrödinger, Roger Penrose

As we shall presently see, incredibly small groups of atoms, much too small to display exact statistical laws, do play a dominating role in the very orderly and lawful events within a living organism.
What Is Life?: with "Mind and Matter" and "Autobiographical Sketches" by Erwin Schrödinger, Roger Penrose

How can we, from the point of view of statistical physics, reconcile the facts that the gene structure seems to involve only a comparatively small number of atoms (of the order of 1,000 and possibly much less), and that nevertheless it displays a most regular and lawful activity - with a durability or permanence that borders upon the miraculous?
What Is Life?: with "Mind and Matter" and "Autobiographical Sketches" by Erwin Schrödinger, Roger Penrose

Nevertheless, the one and only thing of paramount interest to us in ourselves is, that we feel and think and perceive.
What Is Life?: with "Mind and Matter" and "Autobiographical Sketches" by Erwin Schrödinger, Roger Penrose

Wolfgang Pauli

Prize Motivation: "*for the discovery of the Exclusion Principle, also called the Pauli Principle*"
Prize Year: *1945*
Prize Category: *Physics*
Source: nobelprize.org

I don't mind your thinking slowly; I mind your publishing faster than you think.
As quoted in The Harvest of a Quiet Eye : A Selection of Scientific Quotations (1977) by Alan Lindsay Mackay, p. 117

When I was young, I thought I was the best formalist of my time. I thought I was a revolutionary. When the big problems would come, I would solve them and write about them. The big problems came and passed by, others solved them and wrote about them. I was a classicist and not a revolutionary.
As quoted in Faust in Copenhagen (2007) by Gino Segrè, p. 130.5, which cites The Historical Development of Quantum Theory (1982) by Jagdish Mehra and Helmut Rechenberg, vol 1 of 4, p. xxiv, and Inward Bound (1986) by Abraham Pais, p. 186

The layman always means, when he says "reality" that he is speaking of something self-evidently known; whereas to me it seems the most important and exceedingly difficult task of our time is to work on the construction of a new idea of reality.
Letter to Markus Fierz (12 August 1948), as quoted in The Innermost Kernel : Depth Psychology and Quantum Physics : Wolfgang Pauli's Dialogue with C. G. Jung (2005) by Suzanne Gieser

The purely psychological interpretation only apprehends half of the matter. The other half is the revealing of the archetypal basis of the terms actually applied in modern physics. What the final method of observation must see in the production of "background physics" through the unconscious of modern man is a directing of objective toward a future description of nature that uniformly comprises physis and psyche, a form of description that at the moment we are experiencing only in a prescientific phase. To achieve such a uniform description of nature, it appears to be essential to have recourse to the archetypal background of the scientific terms and concepts.
Letter to Carl Jung, (16 June 1948)

Later, however, I came to recognize the objective nature of these dreams or fantasies ... Thus it was that I gradually came to acknowledge that such fantasies or dreams are neither meaningless nor purely arbitrary but rather convey a sort of "second meaning" of the terms applied.
After having dreams about physical terms, which he initially dismissed as a "misuse of physics terminology" by the unconscious, in a letter to Carl Jung (16 June 1948)

I have done a terrible thing, I have postulated a particle that cannot be detected.

Statement of 1930, after postulating the existence of the very elusive neutrino; as quoted by Frederick Reines, in his "Foreword" to Spaceship Neutrino (1992) by Christine Sutton, p. xi

I confess, that very different from you, I do find sometimes scientific inspiration in mysticism ... but this is counterbalanced by an immediate sense for mathematics.

Letter to Niels Bohr (1955). Quoted in Robert J. Scully, The Demon and the Quantum (2007), 7.

Physics is very muddled again at the moment; it is much too hard for me anyway, and I wish I were a movie comedian or something like that and had never heard anything about physics.

Letter to R. Kronig (21 May 1925). Quoted in R. Kronig, 'The Turning Point', in M. Fierz and V. F. Weisskopf (eds.), Theoretical Physics in the Twentieth Century. A Memorial Volume to Wolfgang Pauli (1960),as trans. in M. Klein, Letters on Wave Mechanics, x.

Do we lay our mental screen over reality or is it reality that forces itself on us and compels us to insight (projection or introjection)?

The Innermost Kernel: Depth Psychology and Quantum Physics. Wolfgang Pauli's Dialogue with C.G. Jung by Suzanne Gieser

The state of tension between known and unknown gives the symbol a numinous character, which lends it a power of attraction.

The Innermost Kernel: Depth Psychology and Quantum Physics. Wolfgang Pauli's Dialogue with C.G. Jung by Suzanne Gieser

Eugene Paul Wigner

Prize Motivation: "*for his contributions to the theory of the atomic nucleus and the elementary particles, particularly through the discovery and application of fundamental symmetry principles*"
Prize Year: *1963*
Prize Category: *Physics*
Source: nobelprize.org

It is nice to know that the computer understands the problem, but I would like to understand it, too.
When confronted with the computer-generated results of a quantum-mechanics calculation.

The full meaning of life, the collective meaning of all human desires, is fundamentally a mystery beyond our grasp. As a young man, I chafed at this state of affairs. But by now I have made peace with it. I even feel a certain honor to be associated with such a mystery.
Near the end of his life, Wigner's thoughts turned more philosophical. In his memoirs,

I never expected to get my name in the newspapers without doing something wicked.
In 1963, Wigner was awarded the Nobel Prize in Physics. Wigner professed to never have considered the possibility that this might occur.

In science, it is not speed that is the most important. It is the dedication, the commitment, the interest and the will to know something and to understand it — these are the things that come first.
in an interview by István Kardos (1978). Scientists face to face. Corvina Kiadó. p. 370. ISBN 963130373X.

The miracle of the appropriateness of the language of mathematics for the formulation of the laws of physics is a wonderful gift which we neither understand nor deserve.
"The Unreasonable Effectiveness of Mathematics in the Natural Sciences," Communications in Pure and Applied Mathematics, February 1960, final sentence.

A possible explanation of the physicist's use of mathematics to formulate his laws of nature is that he is a somewhat irresponsible person. As a result, when he finds a connection between two quantities which resembles a connection well-known from mathematics, he will jump at the conclusion that the connection is that discussed in mathematics simply because he does not know of any other similar connection.
"The Unreasonable Effectiveness of Mathematics in the Natural Sciences," Communications in Pure and Applied Mathematics, February 1960.

Physics is becoming so unbelievably complex that it is taking longer and longer to train a physicist. It is taking so long, in fact, to train a physicist to the place where he understands the nature of physical problems that he is already too old to solve them.
As quoted by Colin Pittendrigh (1971). In George C. Beakley, Ernest G. Chilton, Introduction to Engineering Design and Graphics (1973), 40

The unreasonable efficiency of mathematics in science is a gift we neither understand nor deserve.
Quoted in Robert J. Scully, The Demon and the Quantum (2007), 191.

The world is very complicated and it is clearly impossible for the human mind to understand it completely. Man has therefore devised an artifice which permits the complicated nature of the world to be blamed on something which is called accidental and thus permits him to abstract a domain in which simple laws can be found.
In Floyd Merrell, Unthinking Thinking: Jorge Luis Borges, Mathematics, and the New Physics (1991), 156.

[T]he laws of quantum mechanics itself cannot be formulated ... without recourse to the concept of consciousness.
From essay by Eugene Wigner, 'The Probability of the Existence of a Self-Reproducing Unit', contributed in M. Polanyi, The Logic of Personal Knowledge: Essays Presented to Michael Polanyi on his Seventieth Birthday, 11th March 1961 (1961), 232.

Richard P. Feynman

Prize Motivation: "*for their fundamental work in quantum electrodynamics, with deep-ploughing consequences for the physics of elementary particles*"
Prize Year: *1965*
Prize Category: *Physics*
Source: nobelprize.org

But the real glory of science is that we can find a way of thinking such that the law is evident.
The Feynman Lectures on Physics (1965), Vol. 1, 26-3. In Carver A. Mead, Collective Electrodynamics: Quantum Foundations of Electromagnetism (2002), 1.

For those who want some proof that physicists are human, the proof is in the idiocy of all the different units which they use for measuring energy.
The Character of Physical Law (1967), 75.

If there is something very slightly wrong in our definition of the theories, then the full mathematical rigor may convert these errors into ridiculous conclusions.
Feynman Lectures on Gravitation, edited by Brian Hatfield (2002), 21.

If we want to solve a problem that we have never solved before, we must leave the door to the unknown ajar.
In 'The Value of Science,' What Do You Care What Other People Think? (1988, 2001), 247. Collected in The Pleasure of Finding Things Out (2000), 149.

Nature uses only the longest threads to weave her patterns, so that each small piece of her fabric reveals the organization of the entire tapestry.
The Character of Physical Law (1965), 28. Quoted in William H. Cropper, Great Physicists (2004), 397.

They had wasted all their time memorizing stuff like that, when it could be looked up in fifteen minutes.
"Surely You're Joking, Mr. Feynman!": Adventures of a Curious Character by Richard P. Feynman, Ralph Leighton

You can know the name of that bird in all the languages of the world, but when you're finished, you'll know absolutely nothing whatever about the bird. You'll only know about humans in different places, and what they call the bird. So let's look at the bird and see what it's doing—that's what counts." (I learned very early the difference between knowing the name of something and knowing something.)
"What Do You Care What Other People Think?": Further Adventures of a Curious Character by Richard P. Feynman

For a successful technology, reality must take precedence over public relations, for Nature cannot be fooled.
"What Do You Care What Other People Think?": Further Adventures of a Curious Character by Richard P. Feynman

Science is a way to teach how something gets to be known, what is not known, to what extent things are known (for nothing is known absolutely), how to handle doubt and uncertainty, what the rules of evidence are, how to think about things so that judgments can be made, how to distinguish truth from fraud, and from show. —RICHARD FEYNMAN
Quantum Man: Richard Feynman's Life in Science (Great Discoveries) by Lawrence M. Krauss

The test of all knowledge is experiment. Experiment is the sole judge of scientific "truth."
Six Easy Pieces: Essentials of Physics Explained by Its Most Brilliant Teacher by Richard P. Feynman, Robert B. Leighton, Matthew Sands

Observation, reason, and experiment make up what we call the scientific method.
Six Easy Pieces: Fundamentals of Physics Explained (Penguin Press Science) by Richard P. Feynman

Steven Weinberg

Prize Motivation: *"for their contributions to the theory of the unified weak and electromagnetic interaction between elementary particles, including, inter alia, the prediction of the weak neutral current"*
Prize Year: *1979*
Prize Category: *Physics*
Source: nobelprize.org

The more the universe seems comprehensible, the more it also seems pointless.
Dreams of a Final Theory: The Search for the Fundamental Laws of Nature (1993), ISBN 0-09-922391-0.

It seems that scientists are often attracted to beautiful theories in the way that insects are attracted to flowers — not by logical deduction, but by something like a sense of smell.
Physics Today (November 2005) page 35

One of the great achievements of science has been, if not to make it impossible for intelligent people to be religious, then at least to make it possible for them not to be religious. We should not retreat from this accomplishment.
Address at the Conference on Cosmic Design, American Association for the Advancement of Science, Washington, D.C. (April 1999)

The effort to understand the universe is one of the very few things which lifts human life a little above the level of farce and gives it some of the grace of tragedy.
The First Three Minutes (1993)

Elementary particles are terribly boring, which is one reason why we're so interested in them.
"Elementary particles and the laws of Physics" in The 1986 Dirac Memorial Lectures (1987)

It appears that anything you say about the way that theory and experiment may interact is likely to be correct, and anything you say about the way that theory and experiment must interact is likely to be wrong.
In Dreams of a Final Theory: The Scientist's Search for the Ultimate Laws of Nature (1992), 128.

It is even harder to realize that this present universe has evolved from an unspeakably unfamiliar early condition, and faces a future extinction of endless cold or intolerable heat. The more the universe seems comprehensible, the more it seems pointless.
The First Three Minutes (1977), 154. In Milton K. Munitz, Cosmic Understanding (1990), 270.

We have simply arrived too late in the history of the universe to see this primordial simplicity easily ... But although the symmetries are hidden from us, we can sense that they are latent in nature, governing everything about us. That's the most exciting idea I know: that nature is much simpler than it looks. Nothing makes me more hopeful that our generation of human beings may actually hold the key to the universe in our hands—that perhaps in our lifetimes we may be able to tell why all of what we see in this immense universe of galaxies and particles is logically inevitable.
Quoted in Nigel Calder, The Key to the Universe: A Report on the New Physics (1978), 185.

Principles that we now regard as universal laws will eventually turn out to represent historical accidents.
Dreams of a Final Theory: The Scientist's Search for the Ultimate Laws of Nature by Steven Weinberg

For instance, there is nothing like intelligence on the level of individual living cells, and nothing like life on the level of atoms and molecules.
Dreams of a Final Theory: The Scientist's Search for the Ultimate Laws of Nature by Steven Weinberg

At about one-hundredth of a second, the earliest time about which we can speak with any confidence, the temperature of the universe was about a hundred thousand million (10^{11}) degrees Centigrade.
The First Three Minutes: A Modern View Of The Origin Of The Universe by Steven Weinberg

Leon M. Lederman

 **Prize Motivation:** "*for the neutrino beam method and the demonstration of the doublet structure of the leptons through the discovery of the muon neutrino*"
Prize Year: *1988*
Prize Category: *Physics*
Source: nobelprize.org

The best discoveries always seem to made in the small hours of the morning, when most people are asleep, when there are no disturbances and the mind becomes contemplative. You're out in a lonely portacamp somewhere, looking at the numbers on reams of paper spewing out of a computer. You look and look, and suddenly you see some numbers that aren't like the rest - a spike in the data. You apply some statistical tests and look for errors, but no matter what you do, the spike's still there. It's real. You've found something. There's just no feeling like it in the world.
Discover, 10/81

Part of being a scientist is compulsive dedication, the insistence on working without rest until you get what you're after.
NYT, 10/20/88

Physics is the science of observation, and probably no art is closer to the metier of the practitioner than is photography. How parallel are the tasks! Blend respect for meticulous technique with inspiration in order to expose a small piece of the world. Explain through the eye and the mind how a thing subtle but of great wonder can be revealed ... It all amounts to a glimpse of the world which is on the one hand abstract, ethereal and evocative of varieties of esthetic reactions. On the other hand there is for us physicists the faith in an underlying rationale of crystalline precision ... By this reminder of the essential unity of our fascinations, we may even do better science.
Nojima Yasuzo Exhibit Program, Fermilab Art Gallery, 8-9/79

We are honored for research which is today referred to as the "Two Neutrino Experiment". How does one make this research comprehensible to ordinary people? In fact "The Two Neutrinos" sounds like an Italian dance team. How can we have our colleagues in chemistry, medicine, and especially in literature share with us, not the cleverness of our research, but the beauty of the intellectual edifice, of which our experiment is but one brick? This is a dilemma and an anguish for all scientists because the public understanding of science is no longer a luxury of cultural engagement, but it is an essential requirement for survival in our increasingly technological age: In this context, I believe this Nobel Ceremony with its awesome tradition and pomp has as one of its most important benefits; the public attention it draws to science and its practitioners.

"Leon M. Lederman - Banquet Speech". Nobelprize.org. 15 Nov

I got an excellent free education in New York's public schools -- they were good then (1928-39). Then I got a free college education at CCNY. I went to graduate school under the GI Bill. Then when I got my degree, I was handed t:he finest equipment to do the work I most wanted to do. And now they are giving me a medal. [1965 National Medal of Science] That's really pretty funny.

New York Post, 2/10/66

My children have often asked me why I never received a Nobel Prize. I used to tell them it was because the Nobel committee couldn't make up its mind which of my projects to recognize.

New York Times, 20 Oct 1988.

Physics is not religion. If it were, we'd have a much easier time raising money.

In Leon Lederman and Dick Teresi, The God Particle: If the Universe is the Answer, What is the Question (1993, 2006), 198.

Scientists don't really ever grow up. I read, as a 10-or-so-year-old, a book for kids by Einstein. I think it was The Meaning of Relativity. It was exciting! Science was compared to a detective story, replete with clues, and the solution was the search for a coherent account of all the known events. Then I remember some very entrapping biographies: Crucibles, by Bernard Jaffe, was the story of chemistry told through the lives of great chemists; Microbe Hunters, by Paul de Kruif, did the same for biologists. Also, the novel Arrowsmith, by Sinclair Lewis, about a medical researcher. These books were a crucial component of getting hooked into science.When asked by Discover magazine what books helped inspire his passion as a scientist.

The 1998 Discover Science Gift Guide: Fantastic Voyages Children's Books That Mattered, Discover (Dec 1998).

If the basic idea is too complicated to fit on a T-shirt, it's probably wrong.
Archimedes to Hawking:Laws of Science and the Great Minds Behind Them by Clifford Pickover

Observation and measurement is the ultimate defining activity; the act of measurement itself forces a system to choose one of its various possibilities.
Quantum Physics for Poets by Leon M. Lederman, Christopher T. Hill

Robert B. Laughlin

Prize Motivation: "*for their discovery of a new form of quantum fluid with fractionally charged excitations*"
Prize Year: *1998*
Prize Category: *Physics*
Source: *nobelprize.org*

I realized that nature is filled with a limitless number of wonderful things which have causes and reasons like anything else but nonetheless cannot be foreseen but must be discovered, for their subtlety and complexity transcends the present state of science. The questions worth asking, in other words, come not from other people but from nature, and are for the most part delicate things easily drowned out by the noise of everyday life.
"Robert B. Laughlin - Autobiography". Nobelprize.org. 22 Nov 2012

I did notice during my job talk that everybody understood what I was saying immediately - this had never happened before - and that the audience had an irresistible urge to interrupt, heckle, and argue about the subject matter loudly among themselves during the talk so as to lob hand grenades into it, just like back-benchers do in the House of Commons. Being a combative person I rather liked this and lobbed a few grenades of my own to maintain control of my seminar. I later came to understand that this heckling was a sign of respect from these people, that the ability to handle it was a test of a person's worth, and that polite silence from them was an extremely bad sign, amounting to Pauli's famous criticism that the speaker was "not even wrong."
"Robert B. Laughlin - Autobiography". Nobelprize.org. 22 Nov 2012

Physics graduate schools in America are for the most part set up as a first priority to service federal contracts, not to make fundamental discoveries...Indeed it was, and is, the practice at MIT to admit graduate students directly into research groups on an as-needed basis as a kind of labor pool. It took me a while to fully understand this depressing fact of life, but I eventually did and then proceeded to look for a home in a research group as a means of supporting myself while learning the things essential to achieving my larger ambitions. I had by this time become quite cynical about and suspicious of institutions of all kinds, and I felt that government-sponsored science was no more likely to be immune from economic pressures than business.
"Robert B. Laughlin - Autobiography". Nobelprize.org. 22 Nov 2012

Real understanding of a thing comes from taking it apart oneself, not reading about it in a book or hearing about it in a classroom. To this day I always insist on working out a problem from the beginning without reading up on it first, a habit that sometimes gets me into trouble but just as often helps me see things my predecessors have missed.
"Robert B. Laughlin - Autobiography". Nobelprize.org. 22 Nov 2012

What we are seeing is a transformation of worldview in which the objective of understanding nature by breaking it down into ever smaller parts is supplanted by the objective of understanding how nature organizes itself.
A Different Universe by Robert Laughlin

Physics maintains a time-honored tradition of making no distinction between unobservable things and nonexistent ones.
A Different Universe by Robert Laughlin

A universal constant is a measurement that comes out the same every time. A physical law is a relationship between measurements that comes out the same every time.
A Different Universe by Robert Laughlin

The important laws we know about are, without exception, serendipitous discoveries rather than deductions.
A Different Universe by Robert Laughlin

in science, you gain power by telling people what you know; in engineering, you gain power by preventing people from knowing what you know.
A Different Universe by Robert Laughlin

We believe in universal physical law not because it ought to be true but because highly accurate experiments have given us no choice.
A Different Universe by Robert Laughlin

In science one becomes enlightened not by discovering ways to believe things that make no sense but by identifying things that one does not understand and doing experiments to clarify them.
A Different Universe: Reinventing Physics from the Bottom Down by Robert B. Laughlin

Green plants have been extracting atmospheric carbon (and hydrogen) for a living for three billion years, and they simply aren't going to be out-engineered by a bunch of scientists.
Powering the Future: How We Will (Eventually) Solve the Energy Crisis and Fuel the Civilization of Tomorrow by Robert B. Laughlin

Thus, the geologic record suggests that climate ought not to concern us too much when we're gazing into the energy future, not because it's unimportant, but because the energy crisis will be upon us before we succeed in changing the earth's heat balance in a major way.

Powering the Future: How We Will (Eventually) Solve the Energy Crisis and Fuel the Civilization of Tomorrow by Robert B. Laughlin

If you want to survive, you had better acquire knowledge that empowers you and is therefore potentially dangerous.

The Crime of Reason by Robert B. Laughlin

In economics, by contrast, value is a fiction created by human beings for exchanging goods and services.

The Crime of Reason by Robert B. Laughlin

Economics Nobel Laureates

Milton Friedman

Prize Motivation: "*for his achievements in the fields of consumption analysis, monetary history and theory and for his demonstration of the complexity of stabilization policy*"
Prize Year: *1976*
Prize Category: *Economics*
Source: nobelprize.org

If you put the federal government in charge of the Sahara Desert, in five years there'd be a shortage of sand
Unknown

The free man will ask neither what his country can do for him nor what he can do for his country. He will ask rather "What can I and my compatriots do through government" to help us discharge our individual responsibilities, to achieve our several goals and purposes, and above all, to protect our freedom? And he will accompany this question with another: How can we keep the government we create from becoming a Frankenstein that will destroy the very freedom we establish it to protect?
Capitalism and Freedom: Fortieth Anniversary Edition by Milton Friedman

Fundamentally, there are only two ways of co-ordinating the economic activities of millions. One is central direction involving the use of coercion - the technique of the army and of the modern totalitarian state. The other is voluntary co-operation of individuals - the technique of the market place. The possibility of co-ordination through voluntary co-operation rests on the elementary - yet frequently denied - proposition that both parties to an economic transaction benefit from it, provided the transaction is bi-laterally voluntary and informed.
Capitalism and Freedom: Fortieth Anniversary Edition by Milton Friedman

The kind of economic organization that provides economic freedom directly, namely, competitive capitalism, also promotes political freedom because it separates economic power from political power and in this way enables the one to offset the other.
Capitalism and Freedom: Fortieth Anniversary Edition by Milton Friedman

To the free man, the country is the collection of individuals who compose it, not something over and above them.
Capitalism and Freedom: Fortieth Anniversary Edition by Milton Friedman

...a society which is socialist cannot also be democratic, in the sense of guaranteeing individual freedom.
Capitalism and Freedom: Fortieth Anniversary Edition by Milton Friedman

The view that government's role is to serve as an umpire to prevent individuals from coercing one another was replaced by the view that government's role is to serve as a parent charged with the duty of coercing some to aid others.
Free to Choose: A Personal Statement by Milton Friedman, Rose Friedman

money is whatever is generally accepted in exchange for goods and services —accepted not as an object to be consumed but as an object that represents a temporary abode of purchasing power to be used for buying still other goods and services.
Money Mischief: Episodes in Monetary History (Harvest Book) by Milton Friedman

"If you put the federal government in charge of the Sahara Desert," Milton Friedman once said, "in five years there would be a shortage of sand."
The Last Best Hope: Restoring Conservatism and America's Promise by Joe Scarborough

...Milton Friedman was shown the construction on a massive new canal in Asia. When he noted that it was odd that the workers were moving huge amounts of earth and rock with small shovels, rather than earth moving equipment, he was told "You don't understand; this is a jobs program." His response: "Oh, I thought you were trying to build a canal. If you're seeking to create jobs, why didn't you issue them spoons, rather than shovels?"
The Morality of Capitalism: What Your Professors Won't Tell You by Tom G. Palmer

Douglass C. North

Prize Motivation: "*for having renewed research in economic history by applying economic theory and quantitative methods in order to explain economic and institutional change*"
Prize Year: *1993*
Prize Category: *Economics*
Source: nobelprize.org

I had hoped to go to law school, but the war started, and because of the strong feeling that I did not want to kill anybody, I joined the Merchant Marine when I graduated from Berkeley.
"Douglass C. North - Autobiography". Nobelprize.org. 27 Nov 2012

Institutions are the rules of the game in a society or, more formally, are the humanly devised constraints that shape human interaction.
Institutions, Institutional Change and Economic Performance (Political Economy of Institutions and Decisions) by Douglass C. North

Cooperation is difficult to sustain when the game is not repeated (or there is an end game), when information on the other players is lacking, and when there are large numbers of players.
Institutions, Institutional Change and Economic Performance (Political Economy of Institutions and Decisions) by Douglass C. North

The major role of institutions in a society is to reduce uncertainty by establishing a stable (but not necessarily efficient) structure to human interaction.
Institutions, Institutional Change and Economic Performance (Political Economy of Institutions and Decisions) by Douglass C. North

The actors frequently must act on incomplete information and process the information that they do receive through mental constructs that can result in persistently inefficient paths.
Institutions, Institutional Change and Economic Performance (Political Economy of Institutions and Decisions) by Douglass C. North

Institutions reduce uncertainty by providing a structure to everyday life.
Institutions, Institutional Change and Economic Performance (Political Economy of Institutions and Decisions) by Douglass C. North

The most important message, one with profound implications for restructuring economic theory, is that when it is costly to transact, institutions matter.
Institutions, Institutional Change and Economic Performance (Political Economy of Institutions and Decisions) by Douglass C. North

Institutions are a creation of human beings. They evolve and are altered by human beings; hence our theory must begin with the individual.
Institutions, Institutional Change and Economic Performance (Political Economy of Institutions and Decisions) by Douglass C. North

While the deep underlying source of institutions has been and continues to be the effort by humans to structure the environment to make it more predictable, this effort can and frequently does make for increased uncertainty for some of the players. The development of well-specified property rights, for example, will make the overall environment more predictable but will increase uncertainty for those who traditionally have used the land in question without having formal title.
Understanding the Process of Economic Change (Princeton Economic History of the Western World) by Douglass C. North

Because individuals always have the option of competing with one another for resources or status through violence, a necessary corollary to limiting the use of violence within a social group is placing limits on competition.
Violence and Social Orders: A Conceptual Framework for Interpreting Recorded Human History by Douglass C. North, John Joseph Wallis, Barry R. Weingast

Amartya Sen

Prize Motivation: "*for his contributions to welfare economics*"
Prize Year: *1998*
Prize Category: *Economics*
Source: *nobelprize.org*

Although the socialist economies, including those led by communist parties in various parts of the world, have been beset by economic and political problems (including the ' oppression), the aims and objectives that have previously attracted people towards socialism remain still important as they were fifty years ago. The concepts of social justice are also constantly re-emerged after they were weakened by the difficulties encountered in implementing various projects.
Individual freedom as a social commitment (Ch. 2.5, p. 51)

Although capitalism is, in principle, strongly individualistic, it has contributed in practice to reinforce the trend to integration, because it has made our lives more and more interdependent. Moreover, the economic well-being unprecedented in modern economies that have produced meant that they could be accepted social obligations that previously no one could 'afford'.
Individual freedom as a social commitment (Ch. 2.7, p. 53)

Famines are easy to prevent if there is a serious effort to do so, and a democratic government, facing elections and criticisms from opposition parties and independent newspapers, cannot help but make such an effort. Not surprisingly, while India continued to have famines under British rule right up to independence ... they disappeared suddenly with the establishment of a multiparty democracy and a free press. ... a free press and an active political opposition constitute the best early-warning system a country threaten by famines can have
Poverty and Famines: An Essay on Entitlement and Deprivation

the identity of an individual is essentially a function of her choices, rather than the discovery of an immutable attribute
The Argumentative Indian: Writings on Indian History, Culture and Identity

Development requires the removal of major sources of unfreedom: poverty as well as tyranny, poor economic opportunities as well as systematic social deprivation, neglect of public facilities as well as intolerance or overactivity of repressive states.
Development as Freedom by Amartya Sen

What people can positively achieve is influenced by economic opportunities, political liberties, social powers, and the enabling conditions of good health, basic education, and the encouragement and cultivation of initiatives.
Development as Freedom by Amartya Sen

A defeated argument that refuses to be obliterated can remain very alive.
The Argumentative Indian: Writings on Indian History, Culture and Identity by Amartya Sen

Justice is ultimately connected with the way people's lives go, and not merely with the nature of the institutions surrounding them.
The Idea of Justice by Amartya Sen

Democracy has to be judged not just by the institutions that formally exist but by the extent to which different voices from diverse sections of the people can actually be heard.
The Idea of Justice by Amartya Sen

What matters most is the examination of what reasoning would demand for the pursuit of justice – allowing for the possibility that there may exist several different reasonable positions.
The Idea of Justice by Amartya Sen

Joseph E. Stiglitz

Prize Motivation: "*for their analyses of markets with asymmetric information*"
Prize Year: *2001*
Prize Category: *Economics*
Source: nobelprize.org

Today, the issue is very much saving capitalism from the capitalists, from a form of statism that is far worse in some ways than socialism, something I have called "corporate welfarism" in which the power of the state is used to protect the rich and powerful, rather than the poor and society more generally.
Capitalism, Socialism and Democracy (Routledge Classics) by Joseph E. Stiglitz, Joseph A. Schumpeter

Capitalism can't work if private rewards are unrelated to social returns. But that is what happened in late-twentieth-century and early-twenty-first-century American-style financial capitalism.
Freefall: America, Free Markets, and the Sinking of the World Economy by Joseph E. Stiglitz

The financial sector was supposed to ensure that funds went to where the returns to society were highest. It had clearly failed.
Freefall: America, Free Markets, and the Sinking of the World Economy by Joseph E. Stiglitz

In the world of globalization, global aggregate demand is what matters. If the sum total of what people around the world want to buy is less than what the world can produce, there is a problem—a weak global economy. One of the reasons for weak global aggregate demand is the growing level of reserves —money that countries set aside for a "rainy day."
Freefall: America, Free Markets, and the Sinking of the World Economy by Joseph E. Stiglitz

Wall Street's high rewards and single-minded focus on making money might attract more than its fair share of the ethically challenged, but the universality of the problem suggests that there are fundamental flaws in the system.
Freefall: America, Free Markets, and the Sinking of the World Economy by Joseph E. Stiglitz

This is but one of many ironies that have marked the crisis: in Greenspan and Bush's attempt to minimize the role of government in the economy, the government has assumed an unprecedented role across a wide swath—becoming the owner of the world's largest automobile company, the largest insurance company, and (had it received in return for what it had given to the banks) some of the largest banks. A country in which socialism is often treated as an anathema has socialized risk and intervened in markets in unprecedented ways.
Freefall: America, Free Markets, and the Sinking of the World Economy by Joseph E. Stiglitz

In many cases commercial interests and values have superseded concern for the environment, democracy, human rights, and social justice.
Globalization and Its Discontents (Norton Paperback) by Joseph E. Stiglitz

Globalization can be reshaped, and when it is, when it is properly, fairly run, with all countries having a voice in policies affecting them, there is a possibility that it will help create a new global economy in which growth is not only more sustainable and less volatile but the fruits of this growth are more equitably shared.
Globalization and Its Discontents (Norton Paperback) by Joseph E. Stiglitz

Globalization advances material values over other values, such as a concern for the environment or for life itself.
Making Globalization Work by Joseph E. Stiglitz

One of the reasons that most people may perceive themselves as being worse off even though average GDP is increasing is because they are indeed worse of.
Mismeasuring Our Lives: Why GDP Doesn't Add Up by Joseph E. Stiglitz, Amartya Sen, Jean-Paul Fitoussi

In America, corruption takes on a more nuanced form than it does elsewhere. Payoffs typically do not take the form of direct bribes, but of campaign contributions to both parties. From 1998 to 2003, Halliburton's contributions to the Republican Party totaled $1,146,248, and $55,650 went to the Democratic Party. Halliburton received at least $19.3 billion in lucrative single-source contracts.
The Three Trillion Dollar War: The True Cost of the Iraq Conflict by Joseph E. Stiglitz, Linda J. Bilmes

Daniel Kahneman

Prize Motivation: "*for having integrated insights from psychological research into economic science, especially concerning human judgment and decision-making under uncertainty*"
Prize Year: *2002*
Prize Category: *Economics*
Source: nobelprize.org

Money does not buy you happiness, but lack of money certainly buys you misery.
Well-Being: Foundations of Hedonic Psychology

Human achievement is based on collective intelligence—the nodes in the human neural network are people themselves.
Excerpt from This Will Make You Smarter: Daniel Kahneman and More by John Brockman

Faced with the choice between changing one's mind and proving that there is no need to do so, almost everyone gets busy on the proof.
Heuristics and Biases: The Psychology of Intuitive Judgment by Thomas Gilovich, Dale Griffin, Daniel Kahneman

The gorilla study illustrates two important facts about our minds: we can be blind to the obvious, and we are also blind to our blindness.
Thinking, Fast and Slow by Daniel Kahneman

People who are cognitively busy are also more likely to make selfish choices, use sexist language, and make superficial judgments in social situations.
Thinking, Fast and Slow by Daniel Kahneman

We are prone to overestimate how much we understand about the world and to underestimate the role of chance in events. Overconfidence is fed by the illusory certainty of hindsight.
Thinking, Fast and Slow by Daniel Kahneman

The best we can do is a compromise: learn to recognize situations in which mistakes are likely and try harder to avoid significant mistakes when the stakes are high. The premise of this book is that it is easier to recognize other people's mistakes than our own.
Thinking, Fast and Slow by Daniel Kahneman

People tend to assess the relative importance of issues by the ease with which they are retrieved from memory—and this is largely determined by the extent of coverage in the media. Frequently mentioned topics populate the mind even as others slip away from awareness. In turn, what the media choose to report corresponds to their view of what is currently on the public's mind. It is no accident that authoritarian regimes exert substantial pressure on independent media. Because public interest is most easily aroused by dramatic events and by celebrities, media feeding frenzies are common
Thinking, Fast and Slow by Daniel Kahneman

This is the essence of intuitive heuristics: when faced with a difficult question, we often answer an easier one instead, usually without noticing the substitution.
Thinking, Fast and Slow by Daniel Kahneman

A reliable way to make people believe in falsehoods is frequent repetition, because familiarity is not easily distinguished from truth. Authoritarian institutions and marketers have always known this fact.
Thinking, Fast and Slow by Daniel Kahneman

Paul Krugman

Prize Motivation: "*for his analysis of trade patterns and location of economic activity*"
Prize Year: *2008*
Prize Category: *Economics*
Source: *nobelprize.org*

... politics determine who has the power, not who has the truth.
The Australian Financial Review, 6 September 2010, p.15, "Time for Obama to abandon caution". Also seen in the Sacramento Bee [1]

The raw fact is that every successful example of economic development this past century – every case of a poor nation that worked its way up to a more or less decent, or at least dramatically better, standard of living – has taken place via globalization, that is, by producing for the world market rather than trying for self-sufficiency.
The Great Unraveling: Losing Our Way in the New Century, ISBN 0393058506, pp. 368–9; as cited by Edward Fullbrook at logosjournal, Logos 4.1, winter 2005

The central ideas of economic theory are very simple: They boil down to little more than the proposition that people will usually take advantage of opportunities, plus the observation that my opportunities often depend on your actions and vice versa.
The Accidental Theorist: And Other Dispatches from the Dismal Science by Paul Krugman

It is deeply implausible, even offensive, to suggest that the cause of so much suffering can be something as trivial, technical, and fixable as the failure to print enough money. Indeed, there would be no reason to believe such a silly story, except that it happens to be true.
The Accidental Theorist: And Other Dispatches from the Dismal Science by Paul Krugman

Middle-class societies don't emerge automatically as an economy matures, they have to be created through political action.
The Conscience of a Liberal by Paul Krugman

race is at the heart of what has happened to the country I grew up in. The legacy of slavery, America's original sin, is the reason we're the only advanced economy that doesn't guarantee health care to our citizens. White backlash against the civil rights movement is the reason America is the only advanced country where a major political party wants to roll back the welfare state.
The Conscience of a Liberal by Paul Krugman

I believe in a relatively equal society, supported by institutions that limit extremes of wealth and poverty. I believe in democracy, civil liberties, and the rule of law. That makes me a liberal, and I'm proud of it.
The Conscience of a Liberal by Paul Krugman

"We have always known that heedless self-interest was bad morals; now we know that it is bad economics,"
The Conscience of a Liberal by Paul Krugman

people who have been accustomed to stability can't bring themselves to believe what is happening when faced with a revolutionary power, and are therefore ineffective in opposing it.
The Great Unraveling: Losing Our Way in the New Century by Paul Krugman

The point here isn't that top executives are overpaid, though they surely are; it's that the way they are paid rewards them for creating the illusion of success, never mind the reality.
The Great Unraveling: Losing Our Way in the New Century by Paul Krugman

www.ingramcontent.com/pod-product-compliance
Lightning Source LLC
Chambersburg PA
CBHW072048280526
45788CB00006B/2224